"Cracking New Accounts" may be the least expensive investment you can make to benefit your entire sales team. Even the most veteran salespeople can benefit from the tips and techniques contained in *"Cracking New Accounts."* It is unique from most books written on sales in that it is not industry, product or service dependent.

Wirt Cook, General Manager,
IBM

"Cracking New Accounts" is an invaluable book for everyone in sales—and who isn't in sales! I plan to keep a copy on my nighttable and another on my desk. It's great to read straight through, as well as for dipping into for inspiration, tips, strategies and insights. Terry Booton gives us the benefit of his own experience and in-depth knowledge of marketing and selling. But the book is more than just one person's "selling system." You could call it a distillation of the best information – the accumulated knowledge and wisdom – on the subject of selling. So, use it to deepen your knowledge and understanding of selling. Use it as a quick-reference guide to any marketing situation that you might encounter. Use it as a catalyst for yourself and your staff. It will open your eyes to what selling is all about, and, more important, it will open doors.

Scott DeGarmo, Editor in Chief & Publisher,
Success Magazine

"Cracking New Accounts" is the definitive book on "closing business." Terry Booton's new book is entertaining, compelling and complete. If you can't find enough new ideas to pay for this book a hundred times over, you should seriously consider a career in accounting.

Wilson Harrell, Former Publisher,
Inc. Magazine

"Cracking New Accounts" cuts right to the chase, covering all the nitty-gritty, practical details of getting new clients. It's a must read for anyone who wants to grow in her or his business in these competitive times.

Basia Hellwig, Editor in Chief/Executive Female
National Association for Female Executives (NAFE)

*I really enjoyed reading **"Cracking New Accounts."** Luckily, I read it on an airline trip heading to work with one of our members, an office supply dealer. Boy, did that enhance my presentation. My first thoughts were "why didn't I think of that?" I've been training salesmen for over 25 years and Terry's down-to-earth, logical approach to lead generation and seeing the decision-maker was right on! So simple, so logical and so easy. And, I loved the "free offer." What a way to get someone's commitment.*

Jed Casey, Marketing Vice President,
National Office Products Association (NOPA)

*To say reading **"Cracking New Accounts"** was worth the time and effort to read would be a gross understatement. I've been in sales and marketing for my entire career and thought I knew it all. In reading Terry's book, it did several things for me. One, it reminded me how much I had forgotten. Two, reinforced things that we take for granted and three, provided some creative solutions to getting into seeing decision makers. Lastly, it helps you to differentiate yourself from "your competitors."*

Christopher Dane, Managing Director, Agency Sales Program,
American Airlines

*I have just spent an exciting afternoon reading Terry Booton's **"Cracking New Accounts"** and have reaffirmed my enthusiasm for the Salesperson! He articulates well the "dos and don'ts" of each sales effort sighting clear examples of many possible scenarios. This would be a valuable refresher for even the most seasoned sales professional.*

John C. Laing, Executive Vice President, Worldwide Sales,
Symantec Corporation

i

CRACKING

NEW

ACCOUNTS

Quick Tips and Inside Techniques
To Help You Gain Market Share
and
Close the Sale in Half the Time

by

TERRY L. BOOTON

Published By

ADVANCED MARKETING INSTRUCTION
Marietta, Georgia

Library of Congress Catalog Card Number: **91-72852**

ISBN 0-9633282-0-4
First Edition–Second Printing

Cover Design: King & Associates, Atlanta, Georgia

Dedicated to my mother

Birchie Lea Booton

and

To the memory of my father

Lowell Booton

CONTENTS

FOREWORD

Terry Booton speaks to the theories of selling, but only to the extent that they work in the real world. That, above all else, is why his words are so effective in motivating salespeople.

My marketing students call me after they return to their sales territories just to tell me how effective Terry was in helping them to improve their selling skills. An example is the call I received from one of our salesmen from Houston, Texas. The young man called to tell me that, within two weeks after putting Terry's objection-handling techniques into practice, he was able to close three accounts that had been "stonewalling" him.

Those words are indicative of what Terry imparted to hundreds of sales reps during the past few years. Other comments suggested that Terry's techniques were the most important part of my four-and-a-half-day training program. Terry was with them for only a half day.

It's trite, but nevertheless true — Terry Booton is a Salesman's Salesman!

Joe Davenport
Marketing Training Consultant
IBM Corporation

ACKNOWLEDGMENTS

A special thanks to all my friends who reviewed the material and provided me with constructive input.

Greg Bishop
Tom Brodnax
Mike Lezovich
Miles Murphy
Mary Lynne Reeves

I would especially like to thank Lisa Johnston for the time and effort she spent in editing the book.

Also, I would like to thank my wife, Ginger, for her support and encouragement. And a special thanks to my son, Aaron, who got so excited about my writing a book that he went door to door trying to sell it – long before it was completed and he even knew what it was about. He would tell everyone, "It must be good, because my dad goes all over the country talking about it!"

INTRODUCTION

WHY YOU SHOULD READ THIS BOOK

This book is for all salespeople or for anyone considering going into sales, especially business-to-business selling. All types of sales positions can benefit from the techniques used in business-to-business selling. These tips will have even more impact on those salespeople who sell new business, to first-time customers, for their companies. Several aggressive techniques covered in this book are particularly good for those who have the responsibility of helping their companies gain market share. But even if you are a salesperson who covers and sells only to existing customers, you will find these techniques helpful in combating your competitors, as well as in getting your customers to take action.

If you are interested in reducing the number of calls you make before closing an order, then this book is for you. Each tip and technique is designed to help you increase your productivity and earnings by getting more orders with fewer calls or by increasing your close rate on the same number of calls. You'll find no dull theory or philosophy here. This is not a textbook. It's an easy-to-read "inside guide," adapted in conversational style from my powerful, free-wheeling and highly successful sales training seminars across the nation. It's the next best thing to being there!

Research done by McGraw-Hill and published in their lap report in 1987 indicates that it costs $301 for a salesperson to make an industrial sales call. Today, I have heard that number go as high as $500 per sales call for some companies. Every time a salesperson walks out of an account or a prospect's business without an order, it costs the average company $301 or more in marketing expenses. The cost can be even greater for larger corporations. That's why it is critical for the salesperson to properly qualify the prospect on the first call and bring the sale to closure as quickly as possible without jeopardizing any potential business relationship. Otherwise, marketing costs will drive up product cost or erode the margins on the product's current pricing. Not only that, salary costs are continually on the rise. Increasing the productivity of salespeople is a must if companies are to hold down the pricing of their products and remain competitive.

If you are satisfied with the number of orders you or your salespeople are closing, then you need not read this book. If you effectively handle every objection that your prospect or customer gives you, then you need not read this book, either, especially if you get a commitment to buy every time.

If you are new to sales, these practical, street-savvy techniques will help you become much more productive and successful much more quickly. If you are a veteran salesperson or sales manager, you will discover new ideas that can be incorporated into your present marketing style to magnify your charisma and increase your effectiveness.

Because senior salespeople often become complacent, this book offers a new twist on the basics that will get you fired up again about selling – and help put your productivity back on the upswing.

THE OBJECTIVES OF THIS BOOK ARE VERY SIMPLE:

1. To provide tips on **generating** leads.

2. To improve your ability to **qualify** buyers.

3. To improve your ability to effectively **handle objections**.

4. To improve your ability to **gain commitment** and **CLOSE BUSINESS**.

The key to successful selling is the methodology you use. It's an old axiom in the profession that a good salesperson can sell anything. No matter what the product or service is, **selling is selling**.

This book will give you both the proven methodology and the freshest innovations that work.

Part 1 will teach you how to search out leads. It explores how to best approach, understand and effectively question your prospect and to qualify the person's intent or ability to buy. Better qualification **up front on the initial encounter** will save you an incredible amount of time. When you are in commission sales, time is money. **Working smart and using your time wisely is critical.** Being skilled in qualification techniques will give you the extra time you need to spend with real buyers and not "tire kickers."

I will share the "inside" tips and techniques that will enable you to take a four- or six-call close and reduce it to a two- or three-call close – and substantially enhance your earnings over the next year. If you sell a product or service that should be sold in a single call and your close ratio is low, then these tips and techniques will enhance your close ratio and reduce the amount of time you spend with your prospect or customer. That alone will increase your productivity and earnings.

In Part 2, you will learn how to be quick on your feet in handling objections. As a result, you should dramatically increase your self-confidence and gain more commitments.

Most salespeople don't like objections. If you are one of those people, Part 2 is for you. After reading it, you will better understand that every time you hear an objection, you are actually getting closer to a sale. Surprisingly, you will discover how objection handling can be challenging and even fun once you master how to effectively respond.

Part 3 will show you how to maximize the big payoff – the close. You will learn a dozen different closing techniques that will enhance your ability to get sales.

Throughout this book, I will use the term "customer" simply because everyone knows what a customer is. However, I strongly believe that after reading this book, you should decide if you are going to be selling to **customers** or **clients**. The differentiation I make between the two will be covered in Chapter 1. You also will find the word "he" used in reference to the salesperson. This is due not to sexism, but to my desire to make reading this book as simple and user friendly as possible.

Where Do You Fall on the Scale?

Whether you agree or disagree with certain points in the following chapters doesn't really matter as long as you get one good new idea that you can use to your advantage. Mark Twain once said, "I never let school get in the way of my education." Don't let anything you read in this book get in your way, either. Why? Because we all have different personalities. For example, these are the personality styles described by Wilson Learning Corporation:

Drivers - results oriented, net and to the point, dominating and in control.

Expressives - outgoing, visionary, innovative, risk taking and poor listeners.

Analyticals - detailed, practical and conservative.

Amiables - need to establish relationships, gain reassurance and satisfy everyone.

I personally categorize salespeople in two categories, the "subtle seducers" on one end and the "direct chargers" on the other. All salespeople fall somewhere along that scale. It doesn't matter where, because each type of salesperson can be extremely successful.

Illustration 1

THE
SEDUCERS ——————— SALES ——————— CHARGERS
(PULL)   CONTINUUM   (PUSH)
(ASK)   (TELL)

One thing you need to realize is that if 100 salespeople made a call on the same prospect and used the same set of conditions and circumstances, the call would come out 100 different ways due to our different styles and personalities. Yet, all 100 salespeople could be successful. By the same token, half of the group would probably say that the person was a good prospect, and half would say that he wasn't a prospect at all.

We are all different. That's why you need to first learn the techniques and methodologies and then develop a style that feels natural and comfortable for you. I am not going to suggest that you change your personality or emulate verbatim anything you read in this book.

Ultimately, if you take just **one** good idea from this book and adapt it to your own personal style and personality, then your time reading will be well rewarded. Even more importantly, just one additional sale as a result of reading this book will more than pay for it. In fact, one additional sale may allow you to buy truckloads of copies!

In essence, then, you have the opportunity to incorporate many tips that will help you increase your level of confidence, improve your ability to better qualify prospects, deal with objections more effectively and increase your ability to close business. **I am challenging you** to take some of these techniques and apply them to **your** style of selling.

These techniques are based on over 20 years of experience that I have gained in sales. They have been tried, tested and proven by myself and many others. They have worked for me, and I know they also will work for you.

Although this book may contain examples of products that you do not sell, you easily can apply these techniques to your product or service with a little practice. In fact, once you learn these methodologies, I believe you can sell anything!

Just so you know, I may repeat a few ideas throughout the book for emphasis. Pay extra attention to these key concepts. And enjoy reading the book. If you think the book is good, tell your friends. This is one lead that you may not want to pass on to your competitor.

Now kick back and enjoy yourself as you learn how to make your income skyrocket and have fun doing it.

PART 1

QUALIFYING YOUR PROSPECT

CHAPTER 1

MAKE SELLING YOUR LIFESTYLE

Although selling is one of the most exciting and rewarding professions you can enter, many people detest salespeople. But the fact of the matter is that we are **all** salespeople to some extent, regardless of what our professions may be.

- Parents sell their children on why they need to eat certain foods or act in a certain manner.

- Doctors sell their patients on why they need to take certain drugs or undergo surgery.

- Lawyers sell when presenting their cases to a judge or jury.

- Accountants sell when they try to convince their clients to make an investment for tax purposes.

- Waiters and waitresses sell when they offer you those scrumptious desserts after dinner.

- Teachers sell students on why their courses are important.

No matter what line of business you are in, someone has to sell something – whether it's a product, service or idea – before revenue comes into the picture. Nothing happens in any business until someone sells something.

However, when the word "salesperson" comes up, many people still automatically think of the stereotypical used car salesperson, insurance salesperson or door-to-door salesperson. In fact, there are all types of salespeople. There are great salespeople and those who are not so great. And there are all of those in between.

Selling is Hard Work

To be a really good salesperson, it takes someone who is thick skinned and self-motivated. You need these characteristics to keep going with the amount of rejection you often will encounter. In fact, sales is the only profession I know of where a person gets paid to be rejected!

Don't let yourself become intimidated. **Confidence** and **selling yourself** are the keys to your success. Most of the time, salespeople are successful because they are committed to working hard and are having fun doing it at the same time. They enjoy the challenge of learning something new every day. They enjoy figuring out how to solve problems and being perceived as a valued consultant to their prospects and customers. For them, the excitement of selling and winning makes it more than a job – it's a lifestyle.

Some people think salespeople don't work very much, but a successful salesperson is always working, every hour of every day. You should always be looking for new opportunities. And sell at every opportunity you get. Unlike those who have normal eight-hour-a-day jobs, you may find yourself traveling, working at night and on weekends in order to meet with prospects or customers. That's why it takes commitment to be good at sales. Many times you will find that there are just not enough hours in the day to get the job done because of all the activity you have. If you find that you have too many irons in the fire, that's great! Too many irons in the fire indicate that you at least have a lot of potential.

The question is: **Can you do a quality job** for each of those prospects and bring each opportunity to a successful close? You can if you understand the important underlying concepts that will be revealed throughout this book.

Characteristics of a Great Salesperson

Think for a moment. Can you remember the last time you had an opportunity to deal with a really great salesperson? I bet you can, because the really great salesperson leaves a lasting impression. In fact, you can probably remember almost every great salesperson you have met or done business with over the years. I would also suspect that you bought something from him or plan to if you ever decide to purchase his product in the future.

What was it that made that salesperson stand out among all others? What did he do that impressed you? Was it appearance? Attitude? Knowledge of the product or service? Did you feel that he took the time to fully understand what your needs or wants were, and then matched a product or service to that need?

If you did, it's because that salesperson understood that there are several **basic concepts** that underlie every successful sale before the first call is even made. Think about these basics as you read the next few chapters, and make them part of **your** foundation before you move on to the specific sales techniques in later chapters.

Some people say that you can be a "born salesperson." I don't believe that. Some people do possess certain characteristics that we may associate with the sales profession, but again, all of those people are not necessarily successful. And then there are those who say, "That guy couldn't sell anything. He couldn't even sell candy to a kid who was standing right in front of him with a pocket full of money to burn." But guess what? He turned out to be very good at sales. **The difference between a successful and an unsuccessful salesperson is his approach.**

There are a few characteristics that I believe are essential for a salesperson. **Honesty** and **integrity** are first and foremost. A salesperson also should be self-confident, tenacious, creative and have a high level of energy.

Sometimes it takes more tenacity than you think you have, but you can do it if you have the desire and drive. That is when the ego kicks in and the real salesmanship comes out of you. Desire and drive can only come from within yourself. You have to have the desire and drive to win. Desire is a key element to success. Either you have these characteristics or you don't. If the characteristics are not there, you will never be as successful as you would like. However, some of those characteristics can be developed with a little work. If they aren't developed, you may have a tough time in sales.

Race Horse or Work Horse

If you are an owner or sales manager of a company, you need to hire the best salespeople and customer service staff you can find and afford. These people are usually the first point of contact with your customers and prospects. They project the initial image of the company you run or represent. And they are your first line of defense against losing market share.

It is much easier to sell to an existing customer than it is to generate a new one. So you may want to consider the personal characteristics of the salespeople you hire for the type of selling that needs to be done.

Within the categories of seducers and chargers, there are two more categories salespeople fall into: race horses and work horses. The race horse is quick out of the chute and moves very fast. The work horse is more laid back and performs at a more steady and consistent pace. To gain new business and market share, you need race horses. To cover existing customers, you need work horses.

If you are already in sales or considering sales, you might want to evaluate how your own personal characteristics match these two types of selling environments.

New business salespeople are hit-and-run types who play the numbers game. The more people they are in front of or contact, the better their odds of gaining more new customers. These people usually have the following characteristics:

- Hungry (for something that motivates them)
- Tough Skinned
- Like Recognition
- Self-Motivated
- Hard Driving
- Ego Driven
- Risk Taking
- Tenacious
- Self-Confident
- Competitive
- Want to Win
- Results Oriented
- Creative
- Impulsive
- Imaginative
- Take Pride in their Sales Ability
- Empathetic
- Work Hard and Play Hard
- Money Motivated
- Have a Good Work Ethic
- Persistent

Salespeople who sell to existing customers often will be a little more laid back, conservative and amiable in their selling style. This isn't to say that you have to be one or the other to be successful, but you certainly wouldn't go to the Kentucky Derby and bet money on a work horse, regardless of the odds. At the same time, you wouldn't put a thoroughbred race horse in front of a plow.

Selling is a Process

There is a critical sequence in successful sales. Too often, salespeople start marketing without focusing on opportunity. Think of some of your own past encounters with salespeople. Many times, salespeople try to push a product or service on us before we even understand what the product or service is or how it can be of benefit to us. When this happens, what do we do? Usually, we show little or no interest and try to gracefully excuse ourselves just to get rid of them. This type of salesperson usually fails. As we'll explore in depth later on, you must first take the time to understand the customer's needs or wants and then match your product or service to them.

The proper process is as follows:

- **Lead Generation** – identifying opportunities.

- **Call Preparation** – doing your homework on the person or account in advance of making your initial contact.

- **Making the First Call and Maybe Subsequent Calls** – making the initial phone call or personal contact.

- **Establishing Rapport** – getting the prospect to like you.

- **Determining Needs** – determining the customer's requirement.

- **Qualifying Your Prospect** – determining his ability to buy.

- **Educating Your Prospect** – informing the prospect about your product or service and how it could be of benefit to him.

- **Selecting the Right Product or Service** – matching your product or service to his requirements.

- **Justifying the Acquisition of the Product or Service** – financially showing dollar benefits versus cost.

- **Demonstrating the Product or Service** – showing how your product or service actually works.

- **Making a Proposal for the Product or Service** – providing either a formal or informal written or oral offer for your product or service.

- **Closing the Order** – receiving a purchase order, letter of intent, contract or cash commitment for your product or service.

- **Follow up** – contact after the sale to ensure customer satisfaction. Continuing to nurture, satisfy and develop the customer.

It is much easier to sell additional business to an existing satisfied customer than it is to generate a new one.

- **Continue the Process** – Once the customer or client is satisfied, start the process all over again.

Of course, you may not always go through each of these steps. The number of steps can vary depending on the situation, the opportunity or prospect, the way you or your company does business and the type of products or services you offer.

At the beginning of the process, however, you should focus on the basic needs and requirements. You do this by **questioning** and **listening**, and **listening** and **questioning**. Find out as much as you possibly can about your prospect and his needs. Once you have a full understanding of those needs, address each issue appropriately. If you do, you will soon learn that selling is not that difficult.

Selling is Consulting

A good salesperson can be a valuable asset to his prospect when he has the ability to make sound recommendations that match the right product or service to the needs or wants of the prospect. A good salesperson is able to determine these requirements and show not only how the product or service meets the needs of the prospect, but also why it is the best solution out of all the other products or services that may be considered or evaluated. You want to be able to determine needs in the least amount of time possible, with the least amount of effort. The best way is to start asking questions, which will be covered in Chapter 5.

Having Customers vs. Cultivating Clients

To be the most effective professional salesperson, you also want to be viewed as a consultant. There is a distinct difference between being viewed as a salesperson versus a consultant. Salespeople have customers and consultants have clients. What is the difference?

Customers typically make a one-time buy from you, based on price, delivery, convenience or features. When this happens, the product is typically thought of as a commodity. **Clients** make a decision to buy based on technical direction, product strategy or vendor strategy, predictability and stability of the vendor. Customers typically are buying a product. Clients are buying a vendor.

There is a difference not only in perception, but in the way the individuals interact with each other. Think about who has clients: consultants, CPAs, lawyers, decorators, etc. The vendors who have clients are more service oriented. Also, once you have been selected as the consultant who has been retained by your client, your competition is virtually eliminated unless you fail to deliver your product, service or support as promised.

I challenge you to think about the way you market yourself, your company, your products and your services. It is far more profitable to have clients than customers, because it costs less to market to existing customers than it does to market to and generate new ones.

As a consultant, your job is to provide solutions to customer problems, no matter how large or how small they may be. It may be as simple as finding just the right color of dress for someone for that special occasion, or it may be arranging financing for a major venture.

So adapt the attitude of being a consultant from the very beginning, because whatever view you take of yourself will be the view that you project to your prospect. If you think of yourself as an inadequate salesperson or believe that you are just there to ring a cash register, then that is the negative message you will send to your potential buyer.

On the other hand, if you project yourself as a consultant and come across as knowledgeable, interested and concerned, then you, your product, your service and your company will be perceived in a totally different light.

Selling is Problem Solving

Do you have a personal problem that you would like to get rid of forever? If someone told you that for a thousand dollars, you would never be faced with that problem again, would you pay the thousand dollars? Usually when I ask that question, people say they would gladly pay the money.

It's no different in business. If you can relieve, solve or eliminate a problem for the person who has the authority to make a decision, then you have a very good chance of getting him to spend money with you for your particular product or service. People don't like problems, and if you can solve a problem, you can be a hero. Let him know that is why you became a salesperson. You are there to help solve problems and satisfy his needs.

The better you are at resolving problems, the more successful you will be in selling.

Selling is a Lifetime Education

Being a professional salesperson is just as rewarding and reputable as being a doctor, lawyer, astronaut or any other profession that is held in high esteem. Selling, too, involves both artistry and skill. **Both** can be learned.

Doctors go through college, then through medical school and residency before they acquire the necessary skills to go out on their own as licensed physicians. Lawyers go to college and law school and then do internships to enhance skills before beginning to practice. These professionals didn't just decide one day to become professionals, and the next day there they were.

It is not any different for you as a salesperson. You must do your graduate work in the field, on the street and in front of prospects **every day** while gaining the necessary skills required to become highly successful. Like becoming a doctor or lawyer, it takes time and experience to earn the title of "Sales Professional."

For example, one of the biggest issues that a salesperson has to learn to deal with is people saying **"NO."** No one likes to be told **"NO."** I include myself. However, I have learned to take it as a personal challenge and get more motivated as a result of someone saying no. It pays to try to make a game out of it. Here's how.

Selling is Exciting

Selling is like playing golf. In a game of golf, it is just you against the course. The more you play the course, the better you get. In sales, it is just you against the competition and the opportunity. The more you compete, the better you get. The better you get, the more you win! You look forward to getting out of bed each morning just to play the game one more time, as opposed to getting out of bed to go to the battlefield and get shot one more time.

A game? Exciting? You bet! In sales, no two days are ever the same, and you can be certain that there is always a new challenge waiting for you just around the corner. That is where your skill comes in to play, as you learn from your prior experiences and apply those experiences to the new situation. Often, it's that challenge that drives you to new heights of ability, accomplishment and confidence.

You also can think of selling as being a game of chess. You make a move; they make a move. You put them in check; they make another move and escape. Yet, before you know it, **CHECKMATE!**

There is nothing more exciting for a salesperson than coming back to the office with a big order. What a high! It is even more exciting if you were competing against other salespeople and their products.

It is sort of like a dog chasing chickens. Once a dog catches a chicken and kills it, he has the taste of blood in his mouth. You can't ever stop him from chasing chickens after that. It isn't much different for a salesperson. Once you bring in that first sale, you can't wait to go back out there and do it all over again. The excitement of bringing an opportunity to a close gets in your blood.

CHAPTER 2

THE SCIENCE OF GENERATING LEADS

Keep the Pipeline Full

Now that you know what selling is all about, you need to have someone to whom to sell something. **The key to cracking new accounts** is having an ample amount of qualified leads that you can be working actively at one time. New account salespeople live and die by the number of active qualified leads they can generate. It is imperative that you keep your pipeline for prospects full.

Even if you sell out of a store front, you must have traffic constantly coming in and out of your store. Traffic is your opportunity.

It is a Numbers Game

Selling is nothing more than a numbers game. Are you still dating or married to the first person with whom you ever went out? If not, then you understand that you usually have to meet a lot of people before you find the right one. You can't get discouraged. It is no different in selling. You need to do whatever it takes to generate ample opportunity. **You have to get and keep your name and yourself in front of as many people as you can.** You have to separate the prospects from the suspects in your territory. You then need to qualify each prospect. Once you have qualified your prospect, you need to turn the opportunity into an order or sale.

Everyone is a Suspect

Everyone who walks into your business is a potential prospect. Even if that person tells you he is just killing time, he still chose your place of business as the place to look around. What caused him to choose your place as opposed to someone else's? What attracted him? Could he be looking for something subconsciously? If he found it, would he make a purchase?

A good salesperson will view every person as a potential prospect until he has had the opportunity to qualify him. Many times the salesperson has to help him realize that he is in fact, a prospect. Otherwise, why did he come into your place of business in the first place? Or, why did he agree to see you? A good salesperson will seize the opportunity to quickly qualify a prospect to determine if he is a qualified buyer.

Where to Find Leads

Leads are the lifeblood of a new account salesperson. Where do you find leads and how do you generate them? You can most likely find the answers below in the business section of your public library in a matter of minutes. You can find answers to questions like:

- How many businesses are located in the state? _____

- What are those industries by SIC (Standard Industry Classification) Code? _____

- What companies are headquartered in the state? _____
  _____
  _____

- What is the name, address and phone number for each company? _____
  _____

- Who is the CEO? _____

- Who is the president? _____

- Who is on the Board of Directors? _____
  _____
  _____

- What is their line of business? _____

- What are their annual sales? _____

- How many employees do they have? _____

- What kind of earnings do they have? _____

- How many locations do they have? _____

- What are the history and projected future of this company?
  _____

- What is the trend for their industry? _____

- What companies make this particular product? _____
  _____

- Who is their competition? _____
  _____

- What are their industry key ratios? _____
  _____

- What are the key publications for their industry? _____
  _____

You can find answers to questions like these and many more, if you just spend a few minutes browsing through the library. Some libraries even have on-line electronic data bases you can use. If not, you can subscribe to many of them directly and access them via your own personal computer. Listings can be found in the Encyclopedia of Business Information Sources and Dialogue. Listed below are just a few of the data bases, indexes and publications you can use to find important background information about different companies and products as they apply to your territory or geographic market.

DATA BASES

DIALOGUE – Lists 300 data bases that can be accessed via a personal computer. Includes an overview of all the industries.

VIEW TEXT – Includes all newspapers on line.

NCOA – National Change of Address. Lists all the permanent change-of-address records filed with the U.S. Postal Service since February 1986. Contains over 40 million records.

DUN'S MARKET IDENTIFIERS – Contains on-line data base with 6,912,000 records, including information on all sizes of companies, even businesses being run out of the home. Contains the company name, address, phone number, zip code, sales, net worth, growth, officers, family tree, employees and square footage of each business.

INDEXES

Business Index – Lists over 900 industry magazines that discuss strategy for each industry.

Newspaper Publishers – Includes publishers such as Atlanta Newspapers, The New York Times and The Wall Street Journal.

Business Information – Traces publication sources. If you want to look up something about a company, issue, area, businessperson, industry or product, this index will point you to the source and date of publication.

Business Collection Issue Guide – Offers a guide to particular issues of a magazine, listed on microfiche.

PUBLICATIONS

MAGAZINES – Run articles or special inserts with all types of rankings and listings of different companies, such as:

SUCCESS GOLD 100 – ALL FRANCHISE COMPANIES
BUSINESSWEEK 1000
FORBES TOP 200 COMPANIES
INC. TOP 500 COMPANIES
THE FORBES 500s ANNUAL DIRECTORY

FORBES TOP 200 COMPANIES
Lists high potential small companies.

INC. TOP 500 COMPANIES
Lists high potential small companies.

FORBES 500 ANNUAL DIRECTORY
Ranks the nation's largest companies by sales, net profit, assets and market value.

(STATE'S NAME) BUSINESS DIRECTORY
Provides business listings by yellow page category, manufacturers by city and product, and businesses by city within the state. For example, Georgia has 233,000 listings.

DIRECTORIES IN PRINT
Lists 10,000 U.S. business and industrial directories and their order information, cost and circulation. Provides national or regional listings with company name, address, phone number, names and titles of key personnel, financial keys, product and services.

DIRECTORY OF (STATE'S NAME) MANUFACTURERS
Provides name, address, phone, SIC code, computer, sales, employees, executive, product and headquarters locations.

DUN'S MILLION DOLLAR DIRECTORY SERIES
Provides detailed information on more than 160,000 of America's largest companies, both private and public. Includes key decision makers, company size and lines of business.

DUN'S MILLION DOLLAR DIRECTORY TOP 50,000 COMPANIES
Covers the top 50,000 companies by net worth. Taken from the Million Dollar Series.

REFERENCE BOOK OF CORPORATE MANAGEMENTS
Gives biographical profiles of principal officers and directors in more than 12,000 leading U.S. companies.

DUN'S BUSINESS RANKINGS
Offers comparative rankings of 8,000 companies, both private and public, within 150 industry categories and within states.

DUN'S REGIONAL BUSINESS DIRECTORY
Includes Dun & Bradstreet's regional business breakout by geography, industry, SIC code and alphabetic cross-referencing. Identifies the top 20,000 firms in retail, wholesale, services and manufacturing markets for each major metropolitan area. Ranks the top 1,000 companies by sales and by employees, along with their SIC code, address and phone number. Also provides the number of locations, name of the parent company, key officers and the year the business was started. Indicates if the company is private or public, the stock exchange where it is traded and the trading symbol. Covers a wider geographic representation than their Microcosm publication.

MICROCOSM
Captures the local economic system on microfiche. Gives a comprehensive listing of all companies in a region's Standard Metropolitan Area with one or more employees. Provides easy access to hard-to-find branch locations, plants and small privately held companies. Covers more smaller companies than the normal D&B listing. Lists the company name, address, phone number, zip code, owner, employee size, number of locations and Dun's number.

(STATE'S NAME) MAJOR HEADQUARTERED FIRMS

Provided by the Chamber of Commerce. Lists company name, address, phone number, executive and title, type of business and SIC code.

(STATE'S NAME) MANUFACTURING PLANT ANNOUNCEMENTS

Lists new manufacturing companies, showing company name, city, product and number of jobs via SIC code.

U.S. INDUSTRIAL OUTLOOK

Covers prospects for over 350 industries. Gives industry reviews and forecast for goods and services, both domestic and foreign. Provides sales, employment, production, average earnings, etc.

PETROLEUM SOFTWARE DIRECTORY

Provides a guide to the latest software available to the industry by application. Lists vendors with complete address information. Gives description of system and language requirements.

ENCYCLOPEDIA OF BUSINESS INFO SOURCES

Contains over 22,000 citations covering more than 1,100 primary subjects of interest. Includes abstract services and indexes, almanacs, yearbooks, bibliographies, biographical sources, directories, encyclopedias and dictionaries, financial ratios, handbooks and manuals, on-line data bases, periodicals and newsletters, price sources, research centers and institutes, statistics sources, trade associations and professional societies, and other sources of information on each topic.

ALMANAC OF BUSINESS & INDUSTRIAL RATIOS

Lists key business ratios by SIC code and size of company. Gives the number of firms in the SIC code, along with the total sales. Shows the industry averages for key measurements of a company's stability.

DUN & BRADSTREET INDUSTRY NORMS AND KEY BUSINESS RATIOS

Self-explanatory.

THOMAS REGISTER

Lists over 50,000 companies with the company profile, product catalog and vendors of product. Great place to find manufacturers of a particular product. Products and services listed alphabetically, along with product index, company profile, address, zip code, phone number, branch offices, asset rating, company officials and a brand name index.

BUSINESS WISE

Profiles businesses by zip code and lists alphabetically with marketing information on each firm by SIC code. Firms are grouped alphabetically by type of business by zip code; by street with their corresponding zip code; by buildings, office parks and shopping centers along with addresses; and by decision makers with title, phone and firm's name. Also lists numeric sequence of telephone numbers, with the firm's name and address. Allows you to target your market by SIC, zip code, employee size, type of location, years in business and business titles.

(STATE'S NAME) BUSINESS

Lists top 15,000 companies outside major metro areas.

ELECTRONIC NEWS FINANCIAL FACT BOOK & DIRECTORY

Provides current and past years, sales in dollars, along with percent of gross. Lists stock prices, earnings per share, price earnings ratio, earning per share projected and actual, and sales over the last four quarters.

VALUE LINE

Provides an investment survey of trends and directions for the industry, along with information about companies that are publicly traded, including: highs and lows of stock prices, targeted price ranges, insider decisions, institutional decisions, sales, cash flow, earnings, P/E ratio, number or outstanding shares, working capital, debt, networth, rating of company's strength, stock stability, price growth persistence and earnings predictability.

DIRECTORY OF CORPORATE AFFILIATIONS

Contains information on mergers, acquisitions and name changes, plus an in-depth view of major U.S. corporations and their divisions, subsidiaries and affiliates. Lists companies on the stock exchanges and Fortune 500. Provides an alpha index and cross references of over 40,000 divisions, subsidiaries, affiliates, etc. Lists over 4,000 parent companies alphabetically with address, phone number, ticker symbol, stock exchange, sales, number of employees, type of business, corporate officers, divisions, subsidiaries and affiliates. Also lists companies by state and city, along with a list of corporate officers.

STANDARD & POORS INDUSTRY SURVEYS

Offers industry outlooks in terms of trends and direction. Gives industry sales and investment information by vendors, along with the hottest products. Compares company operating revenues, net income, return of revenue, return on assets and return on equity. Also provides current ratio, debt/capital ratio, debt as a percentage of networking capital, P/E ratio, dividend payout ratio and yield.

THE KIPLINGER WASHINGTON LETTER

Provides information on the economy, along with the trends and directions of the future and what to expect.

DUN'S CENSUS OF AMERICAN BUSINESS

Gives summary data on the distribution of more than eight million U.S. businesses at the national, state and county level. Useful for people who want to know more about their markets, it answers questions such as: How big is the market place for my product? Where is the greatest concentration of potential buyers? How is the market dispersed geographically? How large are the establishments in those areas? Where should I locate my offices or retail outlets? How large is the daytime working population in a given area?

INDUSTRY NORMS AND KEY BUSINESS RATIOS

Provides a statistical reference for evaluating and comparing financial and industrial performances of business nationwide. Available in directories or on diskette.

MARKET PROFILE ANALYSIS

Furnishes vital consumer and business demographics within every metropolitan area and/or county in the U.S.

Of course, there are many other places to get leads. The rest of this chapter will give you additional ideas for finding leads and gathering important marketing information on those leads.

TELEPHONE PROSPECTING

Someone calling for eight hours a day, five days a week, can contact over 16,000 people per year. It's a great way to qualify a prospect or sell a product without knocking on doors. It can greatly enhance your productivity.

BUSINESS PARTNERS

Your business associates often have a different set of acquaintances and contacts than you have. Share the knowledge.

OUTSIDE LISTS

Many organizations provide a directory or list of members. Check your library for lists like the State Services Register of:

Physicians
Associations
Chambers of Commerce
Manufacturers

Business publications like the Atlanta Business Chronicle produce a **Book of Organizations**, which provides information on professional, civic and hobby groups in the metro area, plus membership size, top officers, addresses, phone numbers, size of staff and fax numbers where appropriate.

Some may also produce a **Book of Lists**, with information on private and public companies.

NEWSPAPERS

Newspapers, especially in small towns, can be an excellent source of information about people and businesses in that community.

BUSINESS MAGAZINES

Magazines, such as **Success** and **Inc.**, that focus on entrepreneurial companies are a good source for understanding what makes a small-company executive "tick" and what small businesses face on a daily basis. They also will help you understand what is going on in certain industries and marketplaces. There are many excellent magazines worthy of reading.

Money	Harvard Business Review
Fortune	Entrepreneur
Nation's Business	Forbes
BusinessWeek	Industry Week

Visit your local newsstand for these publications and more.

INDUSTRY PUBLICATIONS

Most industries have a trade publication that covers everything from A to Z that is going on in that industry today. What are the issues facing the industry? What can companies do to prosper and grow? How can the industry combat foreign competition? Topics like these are often addressed in such publications.

PEOPLE ON PLANES

You never realize how many leads you can pick up on airplanes, especially if you fly business class or first class. Often, the person beside you has an interest or knows someone who may be a prospect. Utilize this great way to network.

FRIENDS

It pays great dividends to have a lot of friends when you are in sales. Your friends have friends who have friends, etc. Take advantage of this network to make new friends and business contacts.

Again, you are networking. Many times it is not what you know, but whom you know, that will cause you to make a sale.

NEIGHBORS

Not all neighbors are close friends, but having even impersonal conversations about companies and people can be a great way to get new leads and pick up information about individuals and their firms.

ACCOUNTANTS

Number-crunchers often have firsthand knowledge about what is going on in their clients' businesses, as well as other businesses in the area.

BANKERS

These guys hold the purse strings in many companies. They know what is happening before it happens and who has the money. They know the companies that are growing and expanding in the community.

LAWYERS

Just like bankers and accountants, the lawyers usually have the inside scoop on a company and know who the power players are.

COMMERCIAL REALTORS

These people can be a valuable source of information about companies that are coming to town. However, since they are in such a competitive market, it may be difficult to get them to give you information unless they really like you and trust you. They fear information may leak to one of their competitors. The commercial realtor often knows months ahead of time that a company is going to locate in a community. Information like this can certainly give you the competitive edge.

CHAMBER OF COMMERCE

Your local Chamber is a good place to find information such as a company name, address, market, number of locations, parent company, parent city and state, senior executive at location and title, product or service and SIC code, phone number and number of employees. The only problem here is that not all companies in an area are members of the local Chamber.

RESTAURANTS

Small-town, local hangouts are a great place to meet local businessmen. Many executives and owners meet at these local establishments for breakfast and coffee to discuss what is going on in the market and town.

TRADE SHOWS

Shows are also a good place to network, see the competition, find new products and meet new prospects. A recent survey showed that 90 percent of all people passing a vendor's booth had not been contacted by anyone from that company within the last 12 months. Rather than standing around socializing and just answering questions at trade shows, you should be qualifying prospects and closing business. It is a time to sell products or services.

DEALERS

If you sell products through a dealer or dealer network, you can often find lead opportunities that need your involvement. You also can try to convert competitive dealers to represent and sell your product line. If your competitive dealers are not happy with their current suppliers or their products, you may have an easy sale.

REVISIT OLD LEAD LIST

You never know when the timing is right for someone to buy. Your old lead list can be a good place to find new opportunity. Maybe your prospects were not interested in the past for any number of reasons, but today could be the right time to drop in on them again. It is like buying a new car. If I own a new car, most likely I would have no interest in buying another one today. However, if I wreck my new car tonight and total it, buying a new car will be one of my top priorities tomorrow. Business conditions can change just as rapidly.

PAST PROPOSAL FILES

Past proposals work the same way as your old lead list. Review the old proposal. Then go make a call to find out why the old prospect didn't buy in the past and see if anything has changed. Make him aware of your product changes or pricing if there have been any. The changes could make a difference and cause him to buy. You never know. Showing up at the right place at the right time can be rewarding.

COLD CALLS

I really like making cold calls. It is by far more personable than calling on the phone, because you can see the person, the company and the surroundings. If you can get an audience with the decision maker, you can usually do a better job of qualifying and have a better opportunity to turn him into a prospect, even though he didn't think he was one before you came in. You will get a lot of rejection, but you also can be more effective in many cases.

LUNCHEON SPEAKER FOR LOCAL GROUPS

Volunteering to speak gives you a good place to network and have people see you on your feet. It is also good exposure for you and your company. If you do not feel comfortable speaking in front of a crowd, invite someone in to speak on your behalf, such as an expert in the field. However, make certain that everyone knows you are the one who is responsible for the appearance.

INDUSTRY DIRECTORIES

Directories list all of the companies that are affiliated with that industry, including company name, address, phone number, county, statistics of facility, owner, executives and titles, sales and number of employees. Depending on the industry, any number of other vital pieces of information can be available.

BUSINESS DIRECTORIES

There are directories for almost every organization. You can find the directory you need in **Directories in Print**. It contains information on the group along with names, address, phone number, executive, sales, employees, product, etc. Information is dependent on the directory. It's a great way to isolate your target markets.

NICHE MARKETING

These are usually a small number of opportunities where almost everyone in the niche knows something about all of their competitors. Use them to find out competitive information.

MAILERS

This is a good method of getting your name in front of prospects. However, you need to target your mailings to a specific audience. Your message should be net and to the point. For example: who you are, what you offer, why your product or service is important, what the benefit to the prospect would be, etc. Or, what the event is, who its intended audience is to be, what they will receive as a result of attending the event, the duration of the event, time and place. Keep it simple, don't make it wordy and always use an attention-getter right up front. Otherwise the mailer is very likely to end up with the rest of the perceived junk mail. Make yours stand out and get their attention.

CENTRAL COMPLEXES

Office parks are an excellent place to maximize your productivity. For example, if you are selling to doctors, you can go to a medical complex, park your car and call on many prospective buyers at one place. It is almost like a trade show, except that you are going to them instead of them coming to you.

YELLOW PAGES

Provides name of companies in a given city or town along with their address and phone number.

PASSING TRUCKS

Often you may notice a truck on the highway advertising their company or product on the side of the vehicle. It may be a company in your territory that you have never called on or heard of before.

NEWS BROADCAST – TV/RADIO

Local and national news broadcasts often feature stories about companies and their executives, good and bad. Either way, it can be a way of getting a name for your next lead. You often can use the news story as an entree to getting in to see the person.

NETWORKING

Probably the best way to get qualified leads is by networking, or interacting with your peers and other salespeople who sell to your prospects. You can network with anyone you know or meet. It pays to have a lot of extra business cards around if you are going to network. You want to make certain that your name gets out, that people have a way of contacting you with information and you have a way of contacting them to share information. It is the old **"buddy system"** way of gaining information and getting in to see a prospect.

REFERENCE FROM PERSON YOU JUST SOLD

There is no better place to find your next qualified lead than from the person who just bought from you. When you buy something that you think is really neat, what do you do when you see one of your friends? Right. You usually tell him about it. Ask your customer if he knows anyone else who might like to acquire your product. You may need to jog his memory by suggesting types of acquaintances, such as golfing buddies, tennis partners, people they go to church with, or people that belong to their same social club, card playing friends, business partners, friends, etc. You never know how many good leads you may obtain from one satisfied customer. If he comes up with a name, ask him to introduce you to that person if possible, or at least call him on the phone and help you set an appointment for a meeting.

Time is Your Enemy

There are only so many hours in any given day. You can physically do only so much. Therefore, time becomes one of your biggest enemies. Your productivity is constantly being eaten into by unexpected occurrences and wasted efforts.

Since time is the biggest enemy of a salesperson, it is imperative that you spend the majority of your time in the closing phase. You must identify the prospects with the highest potential to buy and focus your efforts on those opportunities. If you can get someone else to do your marketing intelligence or prequalify prospects for you, then you can be much more productive by spending your time doing what you should be doing best, **closing qualified prospects**. Then you need a program to market to and manage the other suspects and prospects in your territory or marketplace.

Even though the suspects may not be qualified buyers today, they may be tomorrow. Stay in touch with the suspects and prospects via mailings, phone calls or advertising. Look for other methods of staying in front of your prospects without having to physically be there. After all, **time is money** to a commissioned salesperson. In order to maximize earnings, you want to have as much time as possible to spend in front of qualified opportunities and still stay in touch with your prospects who aren't ready to buy.

How to Get Started

So you ask, "How do I go about all of this?" The remainder of this chapter will help you understand how to get started and use the information you can obtain from the library or other sources.

If you take a selling job or you already have one that places you in an assigned territory, your survival depends on new or existing customers continuing to buy from you and your company. Without question, **you are the difference** maker in whether a territory is productive and profitable or not. As we discussed, productivity begins with having a continuous and abundant supply of qualified leads. This chapter has covered many ways of identifying and generating your leads. Next, I want to discuss what to do with those leads.

Pre-qualifying – Filtering for High-Potential Buyers

If you are assigned a territory, the first thing you want to do is to analyze your territory and determine how many prospects you have and who they are. In other words, what is your maximum opportunity? Once you determine that, you should set some criteria to prequalify those prospects who have the highest probability of buying your product. For example, let's say you are selling a line of jackets and coats. Your territory is Florida and the Bahamas. The number of prospects for winter coats is going to be considerably less than if your territory was in Michigan and Illinois.

Questions you might ask yourself about your territory are:

- How do I determine what my opportunity is? _____
  _____

- Where is my biggest and best opportunity? _____
  _____

- How many jackets and winter coats are sold in Florida and the Bahamas each year? _____
  _____

- What share of the market do we have? _____
  _____

- What is the percentage breakdown of each? _____
  _____

After analyzing your line, you determine that your biggest opportunity is in the jacket line. Ask yourself the following questions:

- Who are the wholesalers and retailers in my territory?
  _____
  _____

- How do I find them? _____
  _____

- Where is my biggest opportunity? _____
  _____

- What are their annual sales? _____
  _____

- Who is the president or owner of the business?_____
  _____

- Who is the store manager or buyer? _____
  _____

- Where is their headquarters? _____
  _____

- Where are their stores located? _____
  _____

- What is their phone number? _____
  _____

- Which area buys the most? _____
  _____

- Who does the buying? _____
  _____

- Is there any piece of the geography more prevalent in buying than others? If so, which ones? _____
  _____

As you can see, there are many questions that need to be answered. Figure out which ones need to be answered first to achieve your highest level of productivity. After all, you can be a lot more accurate with a rifle than you can with a shotgun. That is what you want to do with your territory. Narrow the opportunity down so you can focus on a particular segment or set of prospects. You know what they say. "Ready, aim, fire." They don't say, "Ready, fire, aim." Managing your territory is no different. First you get ready by knowing who they are. Next you select your target market. Then finally, you go after them!

How to Determine Your Opportunity

How do you determine opportunity? Based on the type of product you sell, there may be certain types of prospects that lend themselves to buying your product or service. For example, if your product is a lower quality product and has a lower price point, you probably will have less success in selling to higher priced specialty shops. On the other hand, if your product is high quality and has a higher price point, your opportunity may not be very good with discounters and lower price point stores.

When you have determined the target market for your product, use the SIC (Standard Industry Classification) codes to break out your opportunity sets by type of retailer and distributor and pin-point your target market. For example, if there are 100,000 retail prospects in your territory and 14 distributors, you might want to see how many different types of retailers there are in your territory. You might also want to see what type of distributors you have in your territory.

Let's say there are 90,000 family apparel stores and 10,000 men's and women's specialty stores. Looking at the distributors, you find that 10 are distributors of family apparel and four are distributors for men's and women's specialty clothing.

It would appear that your biggest opportunities are in the 90,000 family apparel and the 10 family apparel distributors. However, if your product is in the specialty line of merchandising, your best prospects are the 10,000 specialty stores and the four specialty distributors.

So where do you begin? You could start in several different ways. One approach is to first use annual sales, number of employees or the number of retail establishments to help you further qualify the opportunity. Let's say you use sales as the number-one selection criteria and the number of stores as your second qualifier.

You can now rank all of your opportunities, from the establishment that has the largest dollar sales to the lowest dollar sales, and then look at the establishments with multiple locations.

Next, look at your distributors. You might want to rank them by annual sales and then by number of employees. The larger distributors will most likely have more salespeople. The question is, do these distributors already have salespeople selling to your 10,000 opportunities? If so, it might be wise to focus on the distributors rather than the establishments. If you can get the distributors to pick up your line and they are already established, you can make four sales calls instead of 10,000. However, you also need to be realistic and understand that even if these four distributors already are established in your territory, there will be many more opportunities out there where they are not involved. Therefore, you can spend your time on those opportunities that are not going to be covered by your distributor.

This example serves as a model to help you think about how you can best cover your opportunity and attack your targeted prospects. Even though you may not sell in the retail market, think about the methodology used here. It will work in any type of territory or market. Learn to work smart and short hours rather than hard and long hours.

If your company doesn't subscribe to a service or provide you with a territory analysis or the type of marketing intelligence we just discussed, you can find many of the answers to your questions in the publications listed earlier in this chapter. Start building your own data base as you work your territory. It is amazing how much information you can gather from your prospects and customers. This approach certainly takes longer, but it will be worth the effort in the long run if you intend to have control of your territory. You just need to decide what data to collect.

Your Marketing Strategy

Once you have made this initial breakdown of your territory, you should then determine your marketing strategy. Use direct mail, hold seminars, do teleprospecting or go cold calling. Each approach can and will work. I strongly recommend that you use a combination of all four for best results. Each has its benefits.

Mass mailing is a good way of making prospects aware of your company, your product and your service. It can be very effective or very ineffective. What makes the difference? For mass marketing to be effective, you need to have a pre-selected set of targeted prospects. Having an accurate data base to mail from will contribute up to 50 percent of the success of the campaign. You then need to present some type of offer that will motivate the prospect to respond. The offer can account for 25 percent of the success. For better results, follow up the mailing with a telephone call to ensure that the material was received. This is also a good way to make your initial contact with a specific individual. If you do a mailing of 5,000 or more, it may not be feasible to follow up by phone. However, if you use a reply card and a reply card comes back, then your prospect has just pre-qualified himself and you should follow up immediately, if not sooner. You now have someone indicating an interest in something.

Mass mailing allows you to cover a lot of territory with little effort, and it is the least expensive way to reach a lot of people. The problem with mass mailing is that your response rate is usually very low, and the amount and quality of information you receive back also are low. You have to really be creative in developing your mass mailing material. You should have an attention-getter right up front to make people want to continue reading the information you have provided. Otherwise, it has a high probability of being viewed as junk mail, and off to the trash it goes. Again, you need to target your audience, compile your mailing list, determine the objective of the mailing, plan your campaign, put it together and mail it out. Then follow up on the mailing. You may be better off doing a manageable number of targeted mailings, rather than a heavy volume that you can't follow up on.

Seminars are very effective when you target your audience. The advantage of seminars is that those who attend have usually pre-qualified themselves by just being there. You can give your sales presentation once for many, as opposed to giving it many times one on one. This tremendously enhances your productivity. The disadvantage of a seminar is that you cannot always give the personal one-on-one attention each prospect deserves. As a result, a qualified buyer may walk out. It is imperative to follow up with all attendees. It can be just as important to follow up with the no-shows as well. Something could have come up at the last minute that kept them from being there, yet they could be just as qualified as if they had attended. Perhaps they were just too busy running their businesses to get away. This is often the case of an entrepreneur. Those are the ones you might consider going to see personally.

When planning a seminar, make certain you give your prospects ample notice so that they can put the meeting on their calendars. Then follow up by phone a week or two in advance of the event to confirm their attendance, and make another confirmation call a day or two before. You might even send them a fax as a reminder the day before or the morning of the event, if the event is to be held in the afternoon.

Teleprospecting is another way of improving productivity. It can be a much better way to seek out new prospects than knocking on doors. It is less costly than face-to-face selling, and you can contact many more people during the same period of time.

A person using the phone eight hours a day, making 10 contacts per hour, can contact over 16,000 prospects per year. This is an excellent method of supplementing cold calls. It helps reduce the sales cycle time, and it can be accomplished through less costly employees. It is just another excellent way of penetrating your opportunity. You don't have to drive from place to place and knock on doors looking for opportunity, as in cold calling.

If you do cold call, you are limited to the number of calls you can make per day. Let's say you can see five prospects in one day making cold calls. Keep in mind that you most likely will not be talking to five decision makers if you cold call. However, for this example we will assume that all five calls are on the decision maker. Teleprospecting from the same list, you could reach 40 prospects if you were on the phone for eight hours and speaking with five decision makers per hour. At that rate, you could contact 200 decision makers per week versus 25. Using 220 working days per year, excluding weekends, vacation, sick days and holidays, you could contact 8,800 prospects teleprospecting versus 1,100 cold calling. A substantial increase in productivity. An increase of 800 percent! I understand the numbers may vary, but these estimates will be close. If you are counting contacts with companies and not getting to the decision maker, your telephone calls can double. Therefore, your contacts can exceed 16,000.

The advantage of teleprospecting is that you can reach a large number of prospects at a lesser cost than cold calling. And you get immediate feedback. Since it is an interactive conversation, you also have the flexibility to redirect the questioning – flexibility that's impossible with a mailing. It is also much more personable.

The disadvantage is that spending long periods of time on the phone becomes monotonous and boring after awhile. Generally, you can't gather as much and as good information as you can on a cold call. And it is more costly than a mailing.

However, you still have to be prepared to make the phone call, just as you would have to be prepared to make a call face to face.

Cold calls are good because you can physically see the business and talk "eyeball to eyeball" with the decision maker. I believe it is easier to establish a relationship with someone you can physically see. You can tell a lot more about the individual when he is in your presence instead of over the phone. You can check him out, and he can do the same with you. You also can gather better quality information about the company. The better the information, the better you can determine if, in fact, he is a qualified prospect. Often, what could have appeared on a telephone qualification call to be an invalid prospect, may turn out to be an excellent prospect when confronted in person.

Cold calling also has its disadvantages. It is far less productive than the phone due to the driving time usually incurred in covering a geographic territory. Therefore, it is far more costly. However, I believe there is a lot to be said for physical presence, and I encourage you to keep it in the equation when deciding which method is best for you.

When making a cold call, as in any type of prospect contact, you need to have an objective in mind. Know where you are going and exactly on whom you will be calling. Know what questions to ask to further qualify the prospect and achieve your call objective. You should:

1. Be ready to discuss and compare products.

2. Be ready to talk price or investment.

3. Be ready to leave appropriate marketing information.

4. Be prepared to provide a list of references for your prospect.

5. Earn the right to gain his business. If you know what you are doing and you are well prepared, it is not that difficult to earn the right.

It all boils down to effective use of your time and what works best for you. Time management becomes a very critical part of your day and how you manage your territory. There are many books on the market today that address time management, as well as a number of seminars. It would be worth investing some of your time to read up on this subject if you have not already done so. LTS/Time Systems of Atlanta is one example of a company that not only offers a very good time management system, but **also will train you** on how to most effectively utilize its system in order to maximize the usage of your time during the day.

Leave the Door Open

At the same time, if you have determined by your qualifying questions that you have a qualified prospect who is interested in your product or service, ask for the order. But, if you don't get it, leave the door open to come back, or create a reason to come back. You need to realize that it may take you several visits to establish the relationship and the credibility needed for him to do business with you.

Taking the Lead by Following Up

Make certain that when you make a commitment to the prospect for anything, **you follow up on it immediately and get back to him on or before the time frame you promised. This is critical.** Just doing this one little thing, immediately following up, will most likely set you apart from many of your competitors.

If you are selling out of a store front and do not do outside sales, these principles and techniques still apply. Once you identify all of your prospects, you can reach them by doing advertising, mailings and phone calls. You can select the set of prospects or geographic areas on which to focus. Once you get them inside your door, you can qualify them, make them aware of your product or service, get them interested (if you haven't already done so through the mailings, advertising or telemarketing) and then close them. Remember, you need lots of leads or traffic to gain **new** customers. More important, you need **qualified** leads.

Just because a suspect is nice to you, it does not mean he is a prospect. He may be wasting your time. Instead of wasting your time, you could be working with a real prospect. As a new business salesperson, you can't latch on and marry suspects or prospects that are not qualified. Qualify their potential and ability to buy quickly. If they are not qualified, move on even more quickly. You can't make a career out of trying to move a suspect to close if he is not a qualified buyer.

In the next chapter, we will take a look at how to make a successful sales call, now that we know who our prospects are.

CHAPTER 3

HOW TO MAKE A SUCCESSFUL INITIAL SALES CALL

Calling on someone for the first time is similar to TV's "The Dating Game." Your prospects are checking you out. You should prepare for your initial sales call by asking yourself the following questions.

THE SEVEN SACRED RULES BEFORE THE CALL

1. **Are you well groomed, well dressed and professional looking?** You should have a friend or peer make an objective assessment. Buy the best quality attire that you can afford. Conservative, not flashy, is a good guideline for dress for most businesspeople. Your appearance does say something about you, and you are selling yourself in most situations. People first buy you and then your product, service or company.

2. **What about your body language?** Always practice good eye contact with your prospect while you speak, as well as good poise, a positive attitude and a high degree of self-confidence. You project self-confidence by the way you carry yourself and by the way you interact with your prospect. Again, have a colleague or your boss do a constructive evaluation after observing you during a joint sales call together.

3. **Do you appear organized and know what you are doing?** You should have any visual aids or other reference material in order and at hand. The acid test here is to ask yourself the following questions:

"Any time someone asks me for anything, can I get it for him immediately or do I know where to go to find it almost immediately?"

"Can I complete or respond to the commitments I have made on or before the promised time frame?"

4. **Can you speak with confidence and authority about your product or service?** Make certain you know your product inside and out. Also, know everything you can about how your product or service compares to the competition.

5. **Are you enthusiastic and upbeat?** Smile! Keep a positive attitude and think about exciting things. Playing upbeat music before making a sales call can often get you fired up.

6. **Are you excited about your product?** Remember, if you can't get excited about your product, you can't expect your prospect to get excited about it. Become a believer in your product or service and understand all of the benefits it offers.

7. **Are you prepared to tell your prospect what you are going to do and then do it?** If possible, give every prospect a little more than he expects. Punctuality and responsiveness are the key here, along with knowing the parameters in which you can operate.

Above all, **always be on time and deliver on time**. That is part of being professional. If you can do that, your job will become much easier. Why? Because all of your customers will be selling for you to their peers and friends. They know they can depend on you. Punctuality alone will set you apart from the vast majority of salespeople. Don't **you** hate it when someone tells you that he is going to do something for you or get back to you, and he never does? Think about that the next time you make a commitment to someone.

All of the above issues are important to how you are perceived. The question is, will you pass the test when prospects are sizing you up and checking you out? Keeping in mind that **YOU ONLY HAVE**

ONE CHANCE TO MAKE A FIRST IMPRESSION! You will never get a second chance. So make that first impression a good one. If you keep your best foot forward, you may never have to worry about personality conflicts. Remember:

THE MOST IMPORTANT PART OF THE SELLING PROCESS IS YOU!

If you were not the most important part of the selling process, your company could just send out catalogs and have prospects check boxes beside the products they desire. Each prospect would mail in the completed order form and have your company ship the product directly to him without ever involving a salesperson. Your company would be a fulfillment center. You are there to make a difference.

Call on the Top Decision Maker

Selling takes two people, you and a decision maker. Many times you will try to see a decision maker on your initial call and get bumped down to talk to someone else at a lower level. Once you get involved with someone who is not the decision maker on your initial call, you may have a very difficult time getting around him to gain access to the real decision maker.

I have a very firm philosophy that I developed after years of sell-ing. **Make certain that you make your initial call on the PRESIDENT.** This is especially important if you are selling big-tick-et capital asset items. It is also very important if your product will or can cause a change in the way the company operates or does business.

• **The president is most likely the one signing the check.** If you can't get to the president, at least **get to the person who has the authority to make a decision**. You want to sell to the per-son who has the ability to either okay or sign the check. Otherwise, you could get stonewalled by some lower level person and waste a lot of time if the president has no intention of buying your product or service for his company. He may even want something different than the subordinate has requested.

41

• The president knows the buying and investment criteria. Even five minutes with the president will help you set the buying and investment criteria and give you direction on how and where to spend your time in the firm and with whom you should be working. Ask the president to personally introduce you to that person so that it appears that the president is behind you all the way. Then seek to gain his commitment that once you bring a recommendation forward and it meets his investment and buying criteria, he will support its immediate implementation.

This process makes it very easy for you to concentrate only on the areas that are important to the purchase decision. It will save you hours of selling effort.

• The president is also the nicest person. I have found that the president is usually one of the easiest people to see, as well as being one of the nicest people in the organization. He or she can afford to be. Here is a helpful hint to remember: If you can solve a problem for the person who has the ability to sign the check, you will usually walk out with an order. The president is the one person in the organization that does have that authority.

LESSONS LEARNED THE HARD WAY

I learned my lesson long ago about calling on the president first. I knew the president of a company where I was trying to sell my product. I was also good friends with the controller. Being good friends with the controller caused me to bypass the president because I knew my buddy was going to take care of me. Right? **Wrong!**

After weeks of marketing to my friend, he told me that he was going to buy a competitive offering instead of my product. After analyzing all the facts, it was clear that I had the better offering. So, I called on the president and asked him if he knew that his controller was going to make a buying recommendation for a particular product for his company. He said that he did.

I informed him that the recommendation was not to do business with me or my company. He was surprised. Why? Because he had assumed that I would be the supplier. He even told me that he would prefer to do business with me. I suggested that he override the recommendation if he truly preferred to do business with me.

His very revealing comment was as follows: "I pay that man good money to make evaluations like this, as well as help run my entire business. If I overturn his recommendation, it would be like cutting off my right hand. I depend too much on him to alienate him. Had you come to me first, I could have done something about it. However, to overturn his decision now would not be wise. I will have to go with whatever he recommends."

• • • •

Even if you do have a friend inside the company, before you call on anyone else in the organization, **CALL ON THE PRESIDENT FIRST.** It will save you time, energy and effort and eliminate a lot of frustration down the road. In fact, that call can be the best five minutes you will ever spend in an account.

• **It's the president's job to grow the business.** Another reason you want to call on the president is because in all my years of selling, I have never had a president tell me that there isn't any money in the budget for my product or service. Why do you think that is? It's because the president's job is to grow the business and increase the company's profitability at the same time. Presidents and CEOs are interested in making money, and everyone else is more concerned in saving money. If you can show the president how your product or service can have an effect on generating revenue, improving profits and cash flow or reducing operating expenses, the president will find the money, even if he has to borrow it.

It is only the people under the president who really focus on budgets. Many times it is in their performance measurement to adhere to budget guidelines. Not only that, if they do request a budget change, they may have to break down walls or climb mountains to make it happen. Quite frankly, it often is not worth that person's time to go through all the hassle it would take to get the budget changed.

• **The president can save you time.** Another reason you don't want to make your initial call anywhere except at the top is because some other people in an organization may tell you they have authority to buy when, in fact, they don't. As a result, they may have you working your tail off for them gathering information, doing evaluations, making comparisons, doing proposals or any number of tasks, while knowing all along that they aren't going to do business with you.

After investing all of this time thinking that you are going to sell something, you finally realize these people do not have the authority to buy anything. Had your initial call been on the president, you would have found this out immediately and could have spent your time with a qualified buyer. It is terrible to say, but the fact is, people will lie to you about their authority to make a decision.

LESSONS LEARNED THE HARD WAY

A good example of what can happen to you when you don't call on the right person and do the right job of justifying your product is what happened to me the very first day I went on quota. I took over an account from a salesperson who had been working with one of the managers and the controller of the company. She told me the president was ready to expand our product line, and all I had to do was to take him the price quotation for the larger capacity equipment and he would place it on order. You can't imagine how excited I was that I was going to get a big order and big commission check right out of the chute.

I got in my car, drove to the account, walked in and introduced myself to the president. I told him who I was and why I was there, fully expecting him to be overjoyed. Much to my surprise, he sat there for several seconds in dead silence. When he spoke, he told me what he was going to do with our products and where he was going to shove them.

Somehow the president and the salesperson were not singing out of the same hymnal. Calmly, I asked him what the problem was. He responded, and then I gave him my interpretation of what was taking place in his account. Then he explained to me once again his position. Needless to say, his position and thoughts were not the same as the previous salesperson's, his manager's or his controller's.

I asked him if he would give us an opportunity to evaluate the situation in detail. Fortunately, he was kind enough to say yes. I know we completely shocked him when we returned with our assessment. We told him that he was exactly right. He didn't need any more machine capacity than he had for what he was doing. Currently, he was utilizing only about 40 percent of the machine's capacity.

We then asked for a planning session off-site to really identify the problems and make recommendations for corrective action. He agreed. The results of that session were unbelievable. After the meeting, he didn't order the model we had previously proposed. He ordered the largest system we had. The reason was simple. We had not originally satisfied the need of the person who made the decision and signed the check. He knew exactly what he wanted, and he wasn't getting what he thought he had bought. To get what he wanted, he now realized what it was going to take to get it and why.

Once we had taken the time to determine the real requirement and he understood what it would take to get what he thought he had originally bought, he didn't have a problem spending the additional money. In fact, the proposal I first brought to him wouldn't even do the job he really wanted to do. Again, it is a matter of everyone understanding the full requirement or need of the prospect and matching the right product or service to satisfy that need. In this example, we were calling on the wrong person at the wrong level and as a result, we almost lost a customer.

This is a good example of why you need to make certain you are satisfying the person who signs the check and be in a position to justify and defend your recommendation.

If you use this approach in making your initial call – calling on the top decision maker – you will find that you can save yourself a considerable amount of time and effort in your selling process.

Attention-Getters

Once you get in to see the top decision maker, you need to be able to say something that will get his attention so that he will want to stop what he is doing and give you a few minutes of his time. Decision makers absolutely do not have the time to see every salesperson who tries to see them. Therefore, your opening line is critical. Ask yourself, "If I were in their position, what would get my attention? Then what information would I need to make a decision?"

What most executives want to hear from a salesperson is a new idea that can help them better manage their business, make money or save money. Retail consumers usually are looking for quality products that are reliable. They at least want price-performing products and services.

Rehearse your attention-getting lines until you have anticipated all possible comebacks from the prospect and have prepared a logical and well-thought-out response. When you can respond in this manner, you will project an attitude of confidence and professionalism that can help gain you credibility with the prospect. Listed in Appendix A in the back of this book are some examples of attention-getters. You can change the words or lines around to meet your particular situation, product or service.

Another technique to gain the prospect's attention and get him involved with what you have to say is to orally **"paint a picture."** Painting a picture makes your explanation more vivid and easier to understand. It can help simplify your point. This technique is particularly good when trying to describe a very complex or technical issue. Remember, a picture is worth a thousand words. Ask the prospect to **visualize** what it could be like to have your product or service. That usually gets him thinking.

CHAPTER 4

A SHORT COURSE IN UNDERSTANDING BUYER ATTITUDES

Your firm has hired you to generate revenue for their company. Now that you understand your mission and are ready to make calls, let's take a closer look at buyer attitudes and how those attitudes can impact your effectiveness. We will take a look at why people buy and hopefully gain a better understanding about how their attitudes can affect buying decisions. Then we will look at some of the most effective questioning techniques you can use to better understand and identify buyer needs and requirements, qualify your prospects and overcome their objections.

We all have an attitude. It is either positive, neutral or negative. A good salesperson should know in the first couple of minutes of a sales call whether the prospect has a positive, neutral or negative attitude. If his attitude is negative, you already know that your opportunity to sell something is very limited. In fact, you may even be asked to leave or get thrown out.

You must be empathetic and be able to deal effectively with buyer attitudes. Neutralizing any negative attitude and then getting the prospect emotionally involved is key to getting and keeping his attention. Get him involved and move the sell cycle forward. If you can turn that negative attitude around, you may just make a sale. One way to do that is to ask the prospect to tell you why he feels the way he does. In fact, many times his reason for not buying ends up being the reason he does buy.

Why People Buy

• **To satisfy needs or wants.** People buy for many different reasons. However, they primarily buy because of some **need** or **want** they have. What are needs and wants? Needs are things that people must have in order to exist or get the job done. They are necessity items. Wants are things that people would like to have, but they don't necessarily need to exist or function.

If a person is hungry and needs food, almost any kind of food will satisfy that need. Let's say you are selling in a grocery store and a person confronts you with the need to relieve his hunger. What are you going to sell him? You could sell him milk, meat, candy, bread, or almost any kind of food to satisfy his need.

However, if you are selling in an auto parts store and the customer needs an oil filter to fit a 1957 Chevy with a 327 engine, then you are going to have to have the exact filter for that engine or you cannot do business. Nothing else will solve or satisfy that need. The solution here must be a specific fit for a specific problem. The brand may not matter as long as it meets the technical requirements.

What if you were the one who went inside to buy the filter and knew nothing about engines or filters? Let's say that you go in and ask for an oil filter and the salesperson brings one out. You pay for it and leave. Then when you try to install it, you discover it doesn't fit. That is when you first realize that there are different sizes of oil filters. How are you going to feel when this happens? Had the salesperson known what he was doing or questioned you further, you wouldn't be wasting your time taking it back for an exchange.

Another important point to remember is this: **PEOPLE BUY EXPECTATIONS**. When we buy something, we have a level of expectation for that product or service. It may be quality, few repairs, low maintenance, durability, or because it's easy to use, easy to care for, easy to trade in, cost effective or any number or other expectations. In fact, some expectations may not even be reasonable, yet they are there. That is why it is critical to understand the prospect's expectation level before you make the sale. If you both understand the expectation level up front and concur that the product should meet that level of expectation, then problems after the sale are less likely. As a result, you have a more satisfied customer. A lot of these expectations come about as a result of a person's upbringing or value system, which is another reason why people buy.

• **The influence of value systems on buying.** Some people buy based on their value system. If you take a person raised in the ghetto and a person raised in affluence and present any subject matter to them, they very likely will have a difference of opinion because of their backgrounds. Expensive to one person is inexpensive to another. A quality product or service to one person may be junk to another. No big deal to one person may be a major problem to someone else. Easy and simple to one person may be hard and complex to another. We are all individuals. We all view things differently and have different levels of expectations.

You can't instantly know the background or personal history of every prospect you meet. However, during the beginning of the call, the rapport-building stage, you can certainly ask probing questions that will give you a good feel for that individual's background and how he might think.

Find out about the person.

1. Inquire about how long he has been in the job, where he was before this job, his prior experience, or where he is going career wise, etc., as it seems appropriate.

2. Find out his likes and dislikes.

3. Try to understand his goals.

4. Find out how he plans to accomplish those goals.

5. Ask him what he sees as the biggest hurdle in accomplishing those goals.

This may help you better position yourself, your product or your service. The more information you have about your prospect and the better you understand him, the better your chances are in doing business. You need to know what makes your prospect "tick" and what **motivates** him.

In addition to needs, some people buy simply because they want the product. As an example, I want to buy a boat. I cannot financially justify the one I want, but I am going to buy it anyway. I am going to buy it simply because I want it, not because I need it or can cost-justify it. This is an emotional decision on my part. Have you ever bought something that way? Do you think some of your prospects make decisions like that? You know they do! By the way, most decisions are based on emotion. That is one reason it pays to sell to emotion rather than overwhelming the prospect with facts.

Keep in mind that if a person just plain wants to do business with you, **he can justify anything**, even if it may not be cost-justified. He may just want the product or service. He may just want to help you be successful. However, this type of sale usually depends on a positive relationship you have developed over time, or it could be like love at first sight. The chemistry may be just right between the two of you from the start.

Selling by Relationship

The single most important fact that a salesperson must realize is that **people buy from people they like and trust**! There is an old saying that "People don't care how much you know, until they know how much you care." Here is a tip: If you really want to enhance your odds of establishing a good relationship, **put yourself in the shoes of the buyer**.

THE GOLDEN RULE OF SELLING

Think about what you would want to know from a salesperson if you were in your prospect's position. How would you feel if you were in his position? Then treat that person the way HE would want to be treated.

Getting in line with your buyer by understanding his needs, wants, attitude and thoughts is fundamental to developing a relationship with your prospect. The more you are in tune with your prospect and his attitude, the better your chances are of establishing a relationship and turning the prospect into a customer as well as a friend.

After you introduce yourself to a prospect, you might even say to him, "I am anticipating a long-term working relationship with you and your company. So let's get started at getting to know each other."

• **Determine if he is buying a product or a vendor.** You also need to realize that whenever someone makes a purchase, that purchase is being made from one of two points of view. He is either **buying a product** or he is **buying a vendor**. If the purchase is being made based on price, delivery and features, then the transaction rests on just buying a product. When a buying decision is based on price alone, the product is generally considered to be a commodity, and a relationship with the vendor is not considered. If you let features become the sole buying criteria for your prospect, you limit yourself to what you can offer. It stops your ability to get creative. You want to have all the options possible available to you when trying to provide a solution to satisfy a need.

An example might be someone wanting to buy a new car. The requirement is for a two-door, because she doesn't want to walk around and check the doors to ensure that they are locked each time she parks. However, if you were to probe a little bit further, you would find that automatic locks would solve the problem. Your sales opportunity has just expanded from two-door cars to all four-door cars with automatic locks. Don't let yourself get boxed in. You want to keep your options open. Selling only to features limits your opportunity.

On the other hand, if a person is buying a vendor, he is willing to pay more for the vendor's stability or service, his marketing or product strategy or his technical competence. He is buying someone who he can depend on and who will be around for years to come. Another important point to remember is this: If a relationship has been established, the details for finalizing a business transaction usually won't stand in the way.

One of the most important points to understand in relationship selling is that once you have established the relationship, you don't have to worry as much about the competition coming in and taking your business, as long as you continue to perform and deliver on time.

• **Turning a mediocre relationship around.** Relationship selling affects customer satisfaction, market share and profitability. More importantly, your profitability. If you don't seem to have the relationship with your prospect or customer that you would like to have, you might ask yourself these questions:

- What is the problem?
- What has caused the problem?
- What impact is it having on me and my company?
- How do I fix it?

A good place to start getting answers to these questions if you don't already have them is to ask your prospect or customer. Ask him questions like these:

- Why do you do business with me?
- What do we do well?
- How or where could we improve?
- If you were the president of my company, how would you change the way we do business with you?

You will be amazed at the answers you get to these questions once you open up the issues. Sometimes you may fear the answer. However, it often takes this type of questioning to really get your relationship established and moving forward. Questions like the prior ones at least indicate that you care, and you can be assured someone will be waiting to see how you respond to the answers. More important, someone will be waiting to see if you do anything positive with the information.

Think about the last time you needed to buy a product. When you went to the store to purchase that product, the salesperson for one reason or another turned you off, made you mad or said something that made you question his knowledge or credibility. Did you leave the store with the product you went there to buy? Probably not. There is no question about it – the salesperson can definitely make the difference.

To have a good relationship you must:

- Start with **trust and confidence** in each other.

- Believe in each other and **know you can be depended on** by the other person.

- Create an **open line of communication** with ongoing dialogue for everyone involved.

- **Listen and understand** what the person is telling or asking you. If you want to get results, it is usually better to ask someone to do something than to tell him to do something.

- And finally (and this is probably the most critical point), seek a **defined and clear understanding** of expectations from everyone involved.

The Ultimate Rule: Use a Team or Partnership Approach

The best tip of all for overcoming objections is: Use a **partnership** or **team approach** to solve the problem. You need to be a part of (and make the other person a part of) solving the problem and making a decision. Isolate the issues and **make the issues the point of focus**. You never want to make the prospect the point of focus if it is a situation where you need to get something accomplished.

Illustration 2

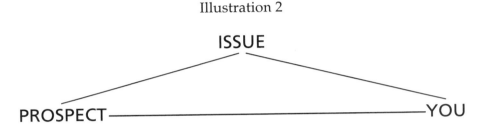

Let me explain what I mean by using this diagram. If you are a sales manager and you call one of your employees into your office to discuss his quota attainment, you may start out by saying something like, "John, you are not making quota."

What position will John most likely take? It will be defensive because you have just made "John" the issue.

What if you had asked John to come in and you said, "You know, John, the company is a little behind on sales. I am not making my quota, and I noticed that none of our team has met his quota objectives. Do you have any ideas how we might fix this problem?" Now you and John are in this together, and the issue is attainment, not John.

Can you see how much more productive the meeting can be when you approach the problem from a "we" point of view, rather than a "you" point of view?

In successful selling, you want to be in it with them. You want to be a part of the solution by helping them solve a problem or by satisfying their needs.

How Well Do You Listen

When you are making a sales call, who is doing most of the talking? Is it you or your prospect? You are there to gather information. The prospect should do most of the talking. Let him finish his statement before you try to interrupt.

You know, God gave us two ears and one mouth. He must have wanted us to listen twice as much as we talk. I don't always adhere to this, but it is an approach that works particularly well in sales. How else will you ever be able to match the right product or service to his needs if you don't ask the right questions?

I have never met a salesperson who admitted that he's a bad listener. However, listening can sometimes be difficult, and often we drift off during a conversation and our ability to hear fools us.

Let me give you an example to test **your** listening ability.

Count from 10 – 1 backwards without making a single mistake. Did you count 10-9-8-7-6-5-4-3-2-1? If you did, you missed it, because counting from 10 - 1 backwards is 1-2-3-4-5-6-7-8-9-10. Had I asked you to count from 1-10 backwards you would have automatically said, 10-9-8-7-6-5-4-3-2-1. Why? Because this is what people ask you to do as a child. Most people miss the answer because they are so conditioned by previous experiences. They have heard that question asked hundreds of times before.

This time, the question was **asked differently** than the way we usually hear it. As a result of our conditioning or not paying attention, we miss the twist and miss the answer.

Do you think this could happen to you when you are making a sales call? Sure it can, and it will. You could be missing the key point that could cost you the sale.

Listen carefully. If your prospect asks several questions in one sentence, rephrase each question one at a time. Then address each question one at a time so that each issue gets covered or resolved.

Don't Overlook the Obvious

As a Sales School instructor, I conducted many practice sales calls with prospective marketing personnel. That is where I would play the role of a customer and grade the student's ability to make an effective sales call. It would drive me crazy when I would ask a question or a series of questions and not get a straight answer. It was even worse when I would get no answer at all. It also would bother me when I would keep throwing out the hint as to what my need or **"HOT BUTTON"** was and the student would never pick up on the clue. Sometimes, I would tell him point blank what it was, and he would still miss it. Why? Because he would either be too busy talking or thinking ahead to his next point or question. He was not **LISTENING** to me as I was trying to explain the problem. As a result of not zeroing in and focusing on my concerns, the student would leave without getting me to commit to anything.

You will be amazed at how easy the selling process is if you just keep it simple. Just ask the prospect the right questions and he will more often than not, give you exactly the information you are looking for. If you involve prospects and let them talk, they will often sell themselves.

Learn to Listen

Listening is a skill. During a conversation, you need to be focused and have 100 percent of your attention on the speaker if you intend on staying up and being fully in tune with the conversation. Why? Studies reveal that you retain only 13 percent of what you hear. So you need to be paying attention to what your prospect is saying. Focusing on listening becomes even more important if your discussion deals with complex or technical issues.

Can you remember a time when you may have had a discussion with someone on any subject, and a day or so later you found yourself getting your head kicked in by that individual because you total-ly missed something that you were supposed to do as a result of that conversation? Worse yet, you forgot the entire conversation? Do you think this happens to you in a call? Sure it does! What about your prospect? You know it does.

Keep the Prospect Focused

How many times is a point made, but it goes over your prospect's head or over your head because one of you was too busy thinking about what you were going to say next? It could have been the key to his buying decision or the key to your selling strategy.

As a professional salesperson, it is your job to accentuate the important points you are trying to get across to the prospect. One effective way of doing this is by **summarizing the important or key points** you have covered. People tend to hear what they want to hear and tune out other issues. Maybe their minds have drifted and they have temporarily gone to the beach. For one reason or another, you may have lost their attention. It is key that you be able to detect this and bring them back up to speed in your presentation.

LESSONS LEARNED THE HARD WAY

A good example of not listening was when a realtor kept showing me houses out of my price range. I told her very clearly the type of house that I could afford. She had predetermined that I could afford a much more expensive house and started showing me more expen-sive homes. Again, I told her exactly how much I was going to spend and asked her not to waste any more of her time or mine. She paid no attention. The next time she took me out looking at houses, she took me to another more expensive home than I was interested in. As a result, I got rid of her and she missed the opportunity for a sale. She was selling what she wanted to sell and not listening to my requirements.

Again, it goes back to listening to the needs or requirements of the buyer and selling within the buyer's parameters and not yours. When you don't listen, it costs you money.

Don't Drag It Out – Net It Out

Another example of not listening would always show up on the final Executive Presentation when I was an instructor in Sales School. That was where all of the students' days of marketing effort were to pay off by asking for the business based on the benefits determined as a result of their study. Usually the night before, the student would spend hours putting together a formal flip chart presentation for his proposal. When he walked in, I would usually ask if he had something that would solve my problem. He would always say yes.

When I asked what it was and how much it would cost, he would say, "I will cover all of that in my presentation." Then I would ask the student, "If you were me, would you buy the product?" He would always say yes. But when I would ask why, he would say, "I am going to cover that in my presentation."

For two and one-half years, I could never get students to net it out for me in plain English without going through the entire formal flip chart presentation. They wanted to show me all the details of what they were proposing. Had they netted it out orally, they would never have had to go through the formal presentation. I had to listen to every single one of the presentations in great detail.

However, here was the interesting thing about the whole situation. A student would come in with a cover sheet and an agenda page. Next came a summary of my current system, followed by details of the proposed system.

Playing the role of an executive, I wanted him to net it out. He wanted to drag it out. Already we had a conflict of interest. When I asked how much it cost, he would answer, "I will get to that later." I would then ask, "What is wrong, are you ashamed of your price?" Sometimes he would turn to the cost page and review the cost benefit analysis for the proposed system. I would then say, "I don't have a problem with that."

Folks, that was a clue to go for the close. However, because that student may have spent six hours and a six-pack the night before putting together all those fancy charts, he was determined to flip back to where he left off and continue with the presentation instead of asking for the order! As I mentioned earlier, it is okay to bypass some or all of the steps when a prospect is ready to buy. You don't necessarily have to go through all the steps of the selling process.

Once he did this, I wanted to see if he was really that slow. I would ask him to please turn back to the cost page and cover the cost one more time. He would explain it one more time. I would say, "That sounds reasonable. I will buy that." You would at least think he would take the hint that I was ready to commit, especially since I said point blank, "I will buy that." But, **NO, NO, NO**. Many students were determined that I was going to see all of those charts of which they were so proud. Believe it or not, many of them would never try to close me once I gave them an indication I was ready to buy. They just wanted to cover their entire presentation.

The point is this. When you are giving a presentation and the prospect gives you the buying signals, **GO FOR IT**! Ask for the order. It is no longer an informative presentation. It is **SELLING** time! If you get a commitment, forget the rest of the presentation. Get a signature if necessary, thank him for his business, tell him what you are going to do next, and leave, unless the prospect requires more. If you don't ask for the order at that point in time, you might screw something up and you may end up leaving without getting the order. Always look for buying signals being transmitted from your prospect to you.

Presenting vs. Selling

There is a big difference between **presenting** your company, product or service and **selling** your company, product or service. In the previous example, it is obvious that the salesperson is more in tune with giving the presentation than getting the commitment and getting out of there. Presenting is good public relations and information exchange, but selling is going for the close. Selling is what generates revenue. Presenting never will. I always consider presenting as "FYI" (for your information). We all know where that kind of information usually goes. It is "Thank you for providing us with that information. We will certainly keep you in mind." It gets filed away under "vendors" or ends up in the trash. We rarely see immediate action as a result of just providing information.

One more tip: Don't get preoccupied with scheduling lots of sales presentations so you can feel like you're doing a good job. All you are doing is keeping busy. Make it a selling presentation if you give one. Salespeople who have mastered quick sales techniques usually don't do a lot of presentations. When they do, it is a selling and closing presentation.

Presenting is a good way to educate your prospect on your product or service. You can do this in a number of ways. You can show him your product. You can tell him about your product or service. You can advertise, have brochures, provide samples, hold seminars or classes, or even have him talk to others using your product or service. You can use any number of methods to educate your prospect. The best approach will vary based on the type of product or service being offered. You will most likely use a variety of methods to educate the prospect.

Once you master the quick qualification technique, which will be covered in a later chapter, I believe you will see a dramatic change in your annual earnings. It is a great approach to very quickly and effectively qualify your prospect right up front so that you can either dig in and close the order or move on to someone else.

As a commissioned salesperson, you cannot afford to waste your time with someone who is not a qualified prospect. Mere **suspects** will never put food on your table or pay the mortgage. They never have and they never will!

Develop an Inside Salesperson

If you are working with an employee other than the decision maker, you might try this. You can say, "Mr. Jones, what can **WE** do to better position ourselves to more effectively present this recommendation to your boss?" Even better, say, "How can I help **YOU** better present the recommendation?" Only use this approach if you feel the person could do a good job selling the product or service for you.

When possible, try to develop an inside salesperson. After all, the person making the decision will probably be more convinced by what his employee tells him than by what you as an outside salesperson say. Try to make certain you get invited to meetings relating to your product or service. You need to be there so you can provide technical assistance or sales support if required. You also may have to step in and clarify certain statements made by your inside salesperson due to his lack of knowledge or inability to properly articulate a particular point. Make sure the inside salesperson is competent and respected before you turn him loose to do your job for you.

Above all, keep in mind that as the salesperson, even if you do have an inside salesperson, it is **your job** to make something happen. Do whatever you can within reason to satisfy needs and wants or solve problems. That is what your job of selling is all about.

You Can't Afford to Throw Away Your Most Valuable Assets

Too often a salesperson will try to match his product or service to a need without fully understanding the exact requirements and as a result, end up selling nothing. Worse yet, he may sell something that doesn't work or satisfy the need at all. When this happens, you generally end up with a dissatisfied customer. As a salesperson, **you can't afford to have an unhappy customer**.

Think about the last time you went to a restaurant and received either poor service or a bad meal. Did you tell your friends? Sure you did! Studies have shown that negative news travels far faster than positive news. In fact, it is said that if a customer is happy with your service, they will tell five people. If they are unhappy with your service, they will tell 10 to 20 people. This could be one reason you may want to be a little more accommodating to your customers when you are trying to satisfy a customer complaint.

In one conversation with your prospect, a dissatisfied customer can destroy the relationship that you may have spent days, months or years trying to build. A bad reputation for a salesperson is no different than the boy or girl in school who has a bad reputation. Word gets out and spreads fast. Everyone seems to know who the person is. Often it is not even true, but the stigma may follow him for a long time. That is why it is important to always take care of your customers. Customers are a company's most valuable asset, and the salesperson is the one primarily responsible for setting the tone and maintaining that relationship. It is the job of a salesperson to get customers and to keep them as customers.

If you have been in sales for a while, can you recall some account that you inherited from someone else? Had everyone and their brother before you tried to sell something to this account, but without success? Then came your turn. You had the opportunity to follow your predecessor and get your shot at the account. The only difference was that this time they bought. What made the difference? Was it you? The fact is, there is a very good chance that you were the difference. When I am selling, I know that I make the difference. I may have been the first salesperson that took the time to really understand the prospect's requirements before trying to actually sell him something. When this happens, I know I will have a long standing relationship with this customer **unless I do something** to sever the relationship.

CHAPTER 5

QUESTIONING FOR RESULTS

Now that you know the basic concepts behind selling and you know on whom to call, as well as how to get their attention, let's get out of the starting gate and get on with executing the initial sales call. In addition to establishing some sort of rapport or developing a relationship on your initial call, one of your main objectives for the first call should be to identify your prospect's need for your product or service and his ability to acquire your product or service. You do this by asking questions. That is what this chapter is all about: asking questions.

A lot of salespeople feel like they spend too much time with a prospect from the time they make the initial contact until the time they close the sale. After all, the less time you spend with a prospect, the more time you have to call on other prospects! That additional time should result in additional sales and commissions.

This chapter is particularly important if you sell a product that has a normally long selling cycle or usually requires you to make numerous calls before you close. My methodology will help you reduce a normal three- to six-call close to a two- to four-call close.

If your selling cycle is a one-call close product or service, this methodology should shorten the amount of time you have to spend with a prospect. If you can figure out how to gather the information you need to make a product recommendation in a shorter period of time, then you will not only shorten the sell cycle, but increase your productivity.

If you learn the methodology I am going to share with you in this chapter, you should greatly enhance your earnings ability, especially if you are in commission sales. This methodology can open doors for you that otherwise may not have opened. It is very effective when calling on an executive. You will easily get him talking about what is on his mind and not yours. Once you get him talking and gain an understanding of his concerns, you can then blend your sales presentation right into the conversation. This is a good way to open the door for business opportunities.

The next three chapters deal with questioning, qualifying and objections. Although each of these elements is very distinct, they overlap considerably. I have sequenced the following chapters in the order of questioning, qualifying and objection handling. However, you never know which element will surface first during a conversation.

Let me clarify this by referring back to the earlier chapter on identifying needs or wants. It may be logical to think that by asking a question you would get an answer to your question. However, instead of an answer, sometimes you may get an objection or counter-question. Therefore, you may need to resolve the objection or answer the question before you can even get in a position to qualify the prospect. Maybe there is a time when you try to qualify the prospect by asking a question or series of questions without first determining his needs or wants, and an objection comes out. Maybe it is a situation where the prospect just hits you with an objection before you even have a chance to open your mouth.

Every Situation is Different

In the world of sales, **THERE ARE NO SILVER BULLETS** that will ensure success every time you try to sell a prospect. So you have to approach each situation differently based on the prospect and his particular needs. There is no cookbook way to make a perfect call, because every call and situation is different. Each salesperson and prospect is different.

Although every situation is different, the one thing that will remain constant is that you will be asking questions of some nature.

They will be questions to determine needs or requirements. They will be questions that will help you qualify their ability to buy or to further draw out, clarify or qualify an objection. As you read through the next several chapters, you will be able to see what I mean by overlap. You will encounter each of these elements in a variety of sequences with different people and situations. In many cases, you can turn the objection around into a closing situation. You may be in a closing situation when an objection will come up and you get to start the questioning process all over again. So don't get all hung up during the next few chapters about sequencing of terminology or examples used.

A successful salesperson finds out if his potential client is a suspect, prospect or buyer by **asking the right questions up front** and by asking the **tough questions up front**. Ask the tough questions up front instead of waiting until you have invested hours, days, weeks or even months with a prospect before you find out he isn't a buyer.

The tough questions are often the ones to which you are afraid to hear the answers. However, they will save you time, energy and effort, as well as make you money in the long run. Your ability to properly qualify your client's ability to buy or to be a potential customer for your product or service can directly translate into increased productivity and earnings for you.

Most people like thinking their own thoughts. Most people don't like to be told what they should think. Therefore, it makes sense to question your prospects in such a manner that their own responses will **bring them to their own logical conclusion**. The decision will appear as though they came to their decision to buy on their own accord, as opposed to having the product or service shoved down their throat by a salesperson. Your job is to help lead them to the best conclusion and not necessarily make the decision for them. Let your prospects do that.

You can start the questioning process by asking more global and general questions up front to help determine needs. Then you can follow up by asking more detailed questions based on the prospect's responses and willingness to expand on those responses. You need to gather enough information to show the prospect that you understand his requirement and gather enough information to determine the right product or service. After you have made the product selection, you need to be able to show him exactly how your product or service can satisfy his need. Once you get good at doing this, you will have more time to spend with other prospects, which should help you increase your sales and earnings.

Therefore, one of the first steps in questioning prospects is to determine if their attitude is one that is positive, neutral or negative. You at least want to get them to a neutral, look-and-listen attitude. You need to get them to a point where they are open-minded enough to listen to what you have to say. Once you move them to a neutral attitude, your chances of successfully moving them to a positive attitude and closing them become even greater.

Getting Your Prospect Emotionally Involved

Your first challenge is to get your prospect's attention. Then you need to get him involved with the sell process. It is **very important** to get your prospect **EMOTIONALLY INVOLVED** with the issue at hand, or with your product or service. The more emotionally involved you can get him with your product or service, the better your odds are of getting him to commit.

We talked about getting the prospects' attention in Chapter 3. Now we need to talk about getting them emotionally involved with the offering. They need to be able to start understanding the opportunity before them and start realizing the potential benefits of your offering. Once you get them emotionally involved, your opportunity to qualify their actual interest in buying rapidly increases. That's because most decisions of any kind are based on emotion.

If you get them emotionally involved from a defensive point of view, you will probably lose. You want them to be emotionally involved with you from a positive point of view, not a negative one.

How do you get a prospect emotionally involved? Some of the ways you can get him involved is by allowing him to be a participant or take part in a demonstration. You can ask him to test or sample your product or service.

Imagine you call a doctor and the doctor suggests that you check into a hospital for tests to determine what is causing your pain. Because you are a procrastinator or think that the pain may pass or you are too busy to take off work, you decide to wait. Later you find out that your decision to wait is going to cost you more because your pain was caused by a hernia that has now incarcerated. As a result, part of your bowel is now going to have to be removed and be replaced with a synthetic tube in an emergency operation.

Had your alternatives been presented more clearly, maybe your decision to not check into the hospital would have been different. Your actions may have changed had the doctor used an attention-getter to get you more emotionally involved with the seriousness of the decision at hand.

What if the doctor had said something like, "This could very well be nothing, and it probably isn't anything. It sounds like you may have a hernia. You might be able to go on for the rest of your life without any complications. However, a certain percentage of cases like this will turn out to be life threatening. It is up to you. Would you like for me to make the arrangements for you to check in tonight or tomorrow?" At this point you may say, "Doc, let's do it now. Tomorrow may be too late."

Some of you may feel this example is threatening or manipulative. Some of you may view it as motivation by fear, but it is your job to sometimes go to extremes to get someone's attention. Otherwise, he could make a career out of deciding to make a commitment. As a result of delaying the decision, it could turn out to be costly for both of you.

What the doctor did in this example was to create a sense of urgency by using an attention-getter to get the patient emotionally involved. He did this by putting the whole issue in its proper perspective. Present your product or service in terms that your prospect can understand. This patient obviously understands the meaning of death and how it can impact his future plans.

Don't Lie or Manipulate

When trying to motivate a prospect to do something, **DON'T EVER LIE** or try to manipulate him. There should never be any need to distort the facts about your company, your product or service in order to arouse an emotion to make a sale. That type of selling will usually come back to haunt you when you least expect it. **Honesty** and **integrity** will win you more business than anything else you can bring to the table.

Your prospects are simply not any different than you and me when it comes to business. We want to do business with someone who we feel will take care of us and handle any problems that may arise. We want someone who will tell it like it is and give us the truthful pros and cons of the product when we ask. We want the salesperson to be our inside salesperson to his company. Getting the prospect involved is just the beginning.

Asking the Right Questions

Don't beat around the bush and appear to be fishing indirectly for information if you are talking to the person who has the ability to make the buying decision. They usually see through that approach very quickly and wonder if you have a hidden agenda. Most people appreciate the direct approach because it gets to the issue very quickly and precisely without wasting a lot of their time. Being direct, up front and asking the prospect how you might help him usually works, especially if he comes to you. I find it is best to be very direct in questioning.

You might ask for a wish list. Ask: "If you could change anything about the way you do _____, what would it be?" Use this question with regard to your product or service. You can even ask if he has a particular need as it relates to your product or service.

If we go back to the example of the 1957 Chevy and the oil filter in Chapter 4, you can see that had the salesperson done the **right** job of questioning the prospect in the first place, he would have found out that the prospect needed a filter for a '57 Chevy with a 327 engine. Then the salesperson could have perfectly matched the exact filter to his exact requirement. If he did not have the right product for his requirement, maybe out of courtesy he could have suggested another place where the prospect might find the product. That would illustrate a much better example of a good salesperson than the example where the salesperson just sold him the first filter at hand. Like the television ad says, "Parts is parts," but we all know that it usually isn't true. There is a difference. Sometimes the difference is significant when we take the time to look deep enough, ask enough questions and fully evaluate all of the aspects of the acquisition. We all know that what we see isn't necessarily always what we get.

What if you took your car to a garage and said to the mechanic, "There is a noise in my car. Would you please fix it?" Then you left. When you returned, you discovered he had taken out your radio. After all, the radio does make noise. How would you feel? That may sound ridiculous, but some salespeople are not much better in their approach to determining the requirements of their prospects.

In the previous example, the line of questioning the mechanic should use to qualify where the noise is coming from could be as follows:

Mechanic: "What kind of noise are you hearing?"

Customer: "A clicking."

Mechanic: "Where does the clicking sound like it is coming from?"

Customer: "The rear."

Mechanic: "Where in the rear?"

Customer: "The wheel."

Mechanic: "Which wheel?"

Customer: "The left wheel."

Now the mechanic knows more exactly where the noise seems to be coming from. You can see how the mechanic funneled the questions until a precise conclusion could be drawn.

By asking a few questions in the right sequence, he may have saved himself hours of trying to locate the noise area. As a result, he can now **increase his productivity** and get the job done more quickly.

Here are some specific direct questions for pinpointing what the prospect's needs or wants might be.

- What are you looking for?

- If you could change anything (from the way it is now), what would it be?

- How can I help you?

- If I were to give you this for free, would you take it? (Then find out why.)

- What is your biggest problem, and what are you doing to fix it?

- Where are you spending most of your time?

- Are you satisfied with your current vendor, product or service? If not, why?

- What value do you feel you are not getting from your current product, vendor, etc.?

- Are you looking for something specific?

- Do you know what you want?

- What do you need?

These are just a few examples of how more specific, directed and open-ended questioning can save you time and money and enhance your relationship with your customers.

Clarify When in Doubt

Many times someone can present something and the other person doesn't have a clue as to what he is talking about. It may be because he is not familiar with the terminology or buzz words. Sometimes a word can have a totally different meaning in two different situations.

When someone uses a term and you think it could possibly have a different meaning, stop him and **verify his meaning** of the word. Don't be embarrassed to ask. It could cost you the business if you miss a key issue or the meaning of a comment. As sales professionals, we need to fully understand what our prospects are saying in order to fully understand their requirements.

Just take a look at the word **"Hit."**

Hit to a baseball player means to safely get on base.

Hit to a street fighter means to physically make contact with someone with the fist or some other object.

Hit to someone in the criminal underworld, on the other hand, has a totally different meaning.

What to Do When You Are Stumped

Have you ever been on a call when the prospect has tossed out a question to you and you didn't know exactly how to reply? Worse yet, you didn't even have a clue as to what the answer was? It happens to all of us at one time or another. Many new salespeople feel like they just have to respond, and as a result, they shoot from the hip, and the answer they give is often incorrect. A prospect may even ask you a question and already know the answer. You never know when you are being tested.

It is always better to say, **"I don't know**, but I will find out and get back to you with an answer right away." If you ever get caught giving a wrong answer when you are being tested by a prospect, you can consider yourself "dead meat" from that point on in the eyes of that person. You will have lost all credibility. If you tell him you will get back to him, do it. But don't make a career out of it! If you are having difficulty in finding an answer, let him know that it may take a little longer than you had anticipated to get a resolution, but you are still working on it. **Don't leave him hanging!**

And don't shoot from the hip! If you don't know, say you don't know. Otherwise, you might just find yourself so far from the facts that you get yourself in real trouble. I know it may be hard for many of you to say, "I don't know," but if you want to enhance your credibility, you must be able to say it.

Open-Ended Questions

How many times has someone asked you a question and you wanted to respond, but you were not certain how you should respond at that exact moment? I am going to give you a technique that tosses the question back to your prospect, and lets you buy yourself time to think about what you may want to say as the prospect continues to explain. This technique will help you gain additional information and keep your composure and professionalism.

Focus on **open-ended questions** that force the prospect to expand on his own thoughts. Open-ended questions require an explanation rather than a "yes" or "no" response. Open-ended questions begin with words like "why," "what," "how," etc. These types of questions give your prospect an opportunity to express in more detail what he is thinking. Here are some examples of open-ended questions you can use:

- What impact would this have on your company?

- What effect would this have on your employees?
- What problems do you foresee?
- What would this mean to your family?
- What do you like about the way you are doing it now?
- What do you like about your current product?

- How would this purchase affect your bottom line?
- How are you doing it now?
- How will management view this proposal?
- How do you plan on paying for the product?
- How will your staff react?
- How do you plan on using the product?

- Why do you ask that?
- Why is that a concern?
- Why do you want to do it that way?
- Why is that important?
- Why are you doing it that way now?
- Why do you like their product?

You are on a fact-finding mission. You are there to find out as much as possible about your prospect's needs and wants, so that you can best match your product or service to his requirements.

Once you ask the question, **LISTEN!!!!!** The response could be your **SIGNAL** to set up for the close.

As you are going through the questioning process, stick to business and **ask questions that make your prospect think**! This will help get him more involved. Try to satisfy each objection before you continue any further. Then go for the close if applicable.

As you should begin to see, the key to gathering information and drawing out objections is to ask a lot of open-ended questions.

THE QUICK SIX – A QUESTIONING AND QUALIFYING METHODOLOGY

Your effectiveness as a salesperson depends on learning a **proven methodology of making a good call**. Then you need to be able to take that methodology and embed it within your own style and personality to make it work effectively for you.

The last part deals with asking for the commitment, or close. Although we have not discussed the close at this point, this is a good place to talk about the technique itself. We will discuss the close in more detail in Chapter 9. The methodology is as follows:

Model Scenario: When Selling a Product

Step 1 IDENTIFY REQUIREMENTS

Fully understanding the needs, wants or problems of the prospect is essential for a salesperson. If you don't fully understand his requirements, how can you effectively match them with the right product? How can you show him how your product meets his need?

An example of quick questioning could include:

- Of all the things you have responsibility for, which ones would you like to give to someone else or eliminate?

- Of all the things that you do during the course of the day, which one would you most like to eliminate?

- If you could change only one thing about the way you ____, what would it be?

- What do you lay awake at night worrying about?

- Of all the responsibilities you have, which one takes up most of your time?

- How can I help you?

- Where are you today? Where are you going? How do you plan to get there? What do you see as your biggest obstacle to achieving those goals?

- Why did you want me to stop by?

- What information do you need to help you gain that additional market share?

- What do you go home and complain to your spouse about the most that goes on here each day?

For example, if you are selling cleaning supplies you might ask:

- Who is really doing the cleaning around here, you or the product, and why do you say that?

- Are your current cleaning supplies doing the work for you, or are you having to provide most of the elbow grease? If it is you, what changes would you like to see take place?

- What do you dislike most about the cleaning supplies you currently use?

- What type of service is your supplier providing you and how do you view the quality of their products?

- What is the toughest item you have to clean?

If you are selling frames for glasses, you might ask:

- What do you dislike most about wearing glasses?

- If you could design your own frames, what would they look like?

77

The product you sell doesn't really matter. What matters is that you are asking open-ended questions that allow the prospect the opportunity to open up and expand the answer to the question so that you can find an area where your product can satisfy the need. You should know in advance the type of questions you should be asking in order to draw out the type of response you seek. After questioning your prospect, you find that **inventory is his biggest problem**.

Step 2 UNDERSTAND THE IMPORTANCE

The second part of your questioning is the most critical part for the prospect. He must know why eliminating the problem, changing the situation or having the product or service is important to him. Again, it is to get him **emotionally involved** with his needs and wants. At this point, many over-eager salespeople start selling their product. However, they still are not in a position to effectively do so.

You might ask:
"Why is inventory a problem?"

Let's say inventory is a problem because it is too high and it is costing money to let it sit there. As a result, turns are less, and carrying costs are eating into potential profits.

Your move, then, would be to gain concurrence that reducing inventory levels would reduce the amount of capital invested in inventory and the cost of money to carry that level of inventory, as well as requiring less storage space and handling.

Step 3 QUANTIFY BENEFITS – PENCIL SELL

The third step of the questioning technique often really grabs the prospect's attention. It is also your second chance to get him emotionally involved if it hasn't happened in Step 2.

Ask your prospect:
"How much would it mean to you financially if you could reduce your inventory level?"

Then ask him to take out a pencil and a piece of paper to help himself and you justify the potential benefit of fixing the problem. It almost always has more impact if the person sees the benefits written down instead of an oral accounting. It also has more impact when the prospects write it down themselves. If it isn't appropriate for them to write it down, let them mentally work through the benefit exercise so it will be their thoughts and not yours. However, you can help guide them.

Once a prospect sees the benefits of addressing the issue, you should trial close for his commitment to do something about it right now. Many times it works and you're done. Other times, he sees the benefit, but for whatever reason he decides to delay his decision to commit. When this happens, you need to figure out some way to not let him leave without doing business with you, especially if the benefit outweighs the cost. Again, this is the time to get creative and come up with another attention-getter.

The facts can be simple to present. Let's say his inventory level is at $1,000,000, and his carrying cost is 30 percent. If he aggressively did something about taking control of his inventory, he could reduce inventory by, say, 10 percent. A 10 percent reduction would get him in line with industry averages, or at least to the point where he would like to be.

A 10 percent reduction of a $1,000,000 inventory is $100,000 dollars, and a 30 percent carrying cost on $100,000 for five years equals another $150,000. This is a total benefit of $250,000 over a five-year period if he were to effectively start controlling inventory – a dramatic result few prospects could resist. The door has just opened for you to trial close.

Step 4 STRESS THE CONSEQUENCE

If your trial close fails, Step 4 reinforces Step 3 by turning the benefit around and presenting it as a lost opportunity. You will now help your prospect understand what it is costing him if he does not do something about the problem now.

Ask: "What is it costing you to do nothing?"

Continuing with the inventory example, if the benefit is $250,000 over five years, that means it is costing $250,000 to ineffectively manage his inventory. That is roughly $50,000 per year; $4,166 per month; $1,041 per week; $208 per day, or $26 dollars per hour to sit back and do nothing. Not to mention that he has just blown about $26 sitting around talking about it!

You then ask: How much longer can you continue to lose $4,166 per month? That is the real issue!

As humans, we hate to lose any of our assets needlessly. Using this approach may give the prospect a different perspective about the issue at hand. He may now decide to commit instead of delaying the decision.

Step 5 SUMMARIZE IMPORTANCE

Step 5 is the easy part. All you do here is summarize and quantify all of the potential benefits the prospect would receive if he did something to manage inventory, not to mention all the other possibilities for improvement in other areas of the business. Use the dollar-benefit amounts with each of the issues where possible. Then ask if he agrees.

Step 6 SEEK COMMITMENT

Then, after you have gained his agreement to the value or benefit of doing something about the problem, move right in to Step 6 and **ask for the commitment** to proceed. If it is appropriate, ask for the order right then and there.

You can take this same methodology and wrap the right words around the situation as it would apply to your particular industry, product or service. If you noticed, however, during the whole **process of questioning**, never once did I mention product of any kind. Neither did I mention any specific features. We discussed the problem. No matter what you are selling, you want to wait until the appropriate qualifying questioning has been done before you even mention your product.

All you want the prospect to do is to realize there is a problem that needs to get solved or resolved. Once you gain concurrence, you will try to gain his commitment to do something about fixing the problem. Once you gain his commitment to solve the problem, you can then start selling your product or service. If you can't qualify him and get him committed to move forward, why should you waste your time trying to personally educate him about your product or try to sell him something? At this point in the call, you might not even know how your product or service will satisfy his need or solve his problem.

Let's use the same methodology, but this time you are going to be selling a service that your company provides. Your company is an engineering firm. The company you are calling on already has a relationship with another firm. I will use an abbreviated version so that all of the details are not rehashed from the previous example.

You **will** see that there isn't any significant difference in selling a product or service when you use this methodology.

Model Scenario: When Selling a Service

Step 1 IDENTIFY REQUIREMENTS

After some discussion, you discover the prospect has been experiencing some delays in getting his engineering specifications completed by their due date or deadline.

You can ask him questions like:

- What would you like to change about your current service?

- What is unacceptable about your current service?

- How would you like to see your current service improved?

- What kind of service would you like to have?

Step 2 UNDERSTAND THE IMPORTANCE

Then ask: Why are delays a problem?

Again, gain his concurrence that the importance of eliminating or reducing delays would save money.

The reason it is important to the prospect is because the delays often cause work stoppage on the project and that can cost wages, lost production and penalties due to an overrun of a completion clause penalty date.

Step 3 QUANTIFY BENEFITS

Next ask: "How much money would you say you are losing per job on the average, as a result of delays?"

The prospect tells you that it can cost anywhere from $500 to $500,000 per project if there is an overrun. Your next question is to determine the average cost per project and the average number of times per year that the incident occurs and establish some annual average dollar costs.

Step 4 STRESS THE CONSEQUENCE

You might ask: "How much is it costing you to sit back and do nothing about solving the problem of having delays?"

Now take a look at what it costs him every time a deadline is missed.

Step 5 SUMMARIZE THE IMPORTANCE

Seek his agreement that he would like to fix the problem. Once he agrees it needs to be fixed, point out to him the track record of your company in meeting deadlines. (Hopefully you have a better story to tell!) Explain what procedures, methodologies, technology, etc., your company uses to help him not miss a deadline.

Even if your rates are more expensive than what he is currently paying, it may cost him less in the long run to hire your firm and not miss a deadline. After your summary, ask him if he agrees. You will need to be able to point out the additional value he will be receiving for the additional expense.

Step 6 SEEK A COMMITMENT

Finally ask him for a commitment to allow your firm to at least work with him on a small project, if not a large one, so that he can get a feel for the type of service, support and cooperation he could experience regularly when doing business with you.

QUICK-SIX SUMMARY CHECKLIST

Each time you make a call, check your questioning progress by running through this checklist. In time, following these six questioning steps will become second nature for you.

1. **Identify** the **needs, wants or problems** of the prospect.

2. Ask right up front **why** that need, want or problem is **important**.

3. **Quantify** the **benefits** or **value** of the opportunity to him.

4. **Clearly state** what happens or what it costs him to do nothing. Stress the **consequence**.

5. **Summarize** the **importance** of an **immediate decision**. Restate the quantified value and consequences, and quickly tie it back to his objectives.

6. **Seek a commitment** at once for him to do something about satisfying the need or solving the problem now. You want to

move the decision process forward in a positive manner by saying, **"Let's take a look and see what we can do."** If it is appropriate, don't waste your time looking, go for the close. Ask for the order.

You can never ask enough questions. Remember that the question that usually trips you up is the one you forgot to ask. Therefore, don't let your best sales calls be made in your mind, in your car, after the call, on the way home or after the prospect walks out the door.

CHAPTER 6

QUALIFYING YOUR PROSPECT

Qualifying the prospect up front is the key to not wasting time. By using a proven methodology, you should enhance your productivity. Use the questioning methodology that we have discussed to first determine needs and wants. Help the prospect understand why it is important and what benefits would be derived if he were to acquire your product or service. Help him understand **what it may cost him not** to have your product or service. Then go for the close. Get his commitment.

When you qualify your prospect, you are attempting to do only one thing: determine his ability and probability of doing business with you. It is that simple.

There are a million questions you can ask in qualifying a prospect. The questions you ask will depend entirely on the type of product or service you offer. Listed below are excellent examples of qualifying questions to help you get started.

- When would you like the policy to be in effect?
- When would you like delivery?
- When would you like to be operational?
- Which color would you prefer?
- Is your annual income greater than $_____?
- Do you currently use a competitive product?
- Do you pay an outside source to do that work for you?
- How much money have you allocated for such an expenditure?
- Does that amount of investment seem reasonable?
- What is your ship to address?
- To whom should I send the invoice?
- Would you be paying cash or charging the item?

- How many would you like?
- Which size do you want to take?
- Who will be making the decision?
- When will you make a decision?
- Is there anything standing in the way of us doing business today?
- Do you currently have a _____?
- Do you ever have a problem with _____?
- If you could improve the way you do _____, would you change?
- Which vendor do you currently buy these products from?
- Do you ever have a requirement for _____?
- If we have it, will you take it today?
- If I could get it today, would you take it?
- If it comes in your size, do you want it?
- Do you have more than _____ employees?
- Are your sales greater than _____?
- Do you own multiple properties?
- Would you change if the change saved or made you money?

The list could go on and on. All you are trying to do is to size up your opportunity to do business. Then determine his ability to buy your product or service. He may very well like to have your product, but either doesn't have the authority or the means to make the acquisition.

One technique I use when someone calls and requests that I meet with him right away is to ask him questions like:

- How can I help you?
- Who will be involved in the decision?
- Who will be making the final decision?
- What is your decision process?
- How much money do you have allocated in the budget for this acquisition?
- What other vendors are you talking to?
- When do you want to be operational?
- When do you want to take delivery?

These may not be the exact questions, because the questions will depend on the product or service. Once I get answers to questions like these, I will usually tell him that I will send him information on my product and suggest that he call one of my current clients for a reference. I will have the prospect ask my client what I have personally done for him and find out how well I supported him as a salesperson. I also will say that when I come to meet with him personally, I will try to have a cost analysis and all of the information he will need to make a decision. Then I tell him, "If I can resolve all of the issues and answer all of your concerns, at the end of the meeting, I am going to ask you to place an order. Fair enough?" **That is a qualifying statement!**

Flushing Out Objections

If he is just a **"tire kicker,"** you will usually find out right then and there because he knows you are going to ask him to buy something when you get there. You will be surprised at what objections or obstacles he may throw out to you at this time. However, that is exactly what you want him to do. You want to qualify him on the phone if you can, rather than waste your time driving or flying to his location to determine he is not a qualified buyer.

When I get there, I will verify that he got the information I sent and called my references. Then I will reiterate: "If I can resolve all of your issues and answer all of your questions, at the end of the meeting, I am going to ask you to order my product or service." If he is ever going to have an objection, you can be certain it will be now. If he gives you six reasons for not buying, you at least know which six are standing in the way of doing business with him, and not the other 20 you may have read into the situation.

The initial sales call is kind of like trying to get a date. You are qualifying your opportunity. Can you remember the last time you were out running around looking for a girl or a guy with whom to spend an evening? I know that may have been a long time ago for a lot of you. Then again, it could have been just last night for a few of you! Let's imagine you walk into a room and see some good-looking guy or gal, but you don't know who they are and there is no one around to introduce you.

What do you do? Don't you find yourself making your way over to that person and striking up a conversation? Don't you start asking open-ended questions to establish some type of rapport and find a common ground of interest?

Once you feel comfortable with the person and find an area of common interest, what do you do? Sure, you go for the **CLOSE**. You try to arrange to get together to do something with the person. What happens then? Right. You may get an objection. Then what do you do? You have two options. You can say, "Hey, I have had enough of this excitement!" Then you can move on to someone else. Or, you can say to yourself, "This still looks like the best opportunity here!" You dig in and try to overcome the objection. Either way, the choice is yours. Hopefully, you try to handle the objection, and then once again, go for the close.

Somewhere during that conversation, you know if you are going to have a chance for a date with that person or not. If you think you have a chance, you continue the conversation and if not, you move on to someone else. What you are doing in essence is **qualifying your opportunity**.

It is not any different in sales. Some people would view the situation as an opportunity and move in for the close. Others would view it as a waste of time and move on to someone else.

In fact, the decision to date in the above example may not be yours to make. You may be either accepted or rejected. You may be told to move on or to get lost. You can walk away at this point, or you can do something to change that initial reaction. The choice now is yours. Either way, the person was qualified.

Asking the Real Qualifier

The next questioning technique might be the most important of all in drawing out objections. It is the one I call the Real Qualifier. It will determine immediately if you have a qualified prospect or not. It is the **"IF"** question. You simply ask something like this:

- If I could solve your problem, would you do business with me?

- If I could show you my product is equal to or better than my competition's, would you buy from me?

- If you can get approval, will you do business with me?

You may have noticed that I ended the qualifying "IF" question, with the word **"ME."** This is important because you do not want to do all the work and then have him go elsewhere to buy the same or a similar product from your competitor. You want to gain a commitment that the prospect is relying on **you** to provide the product or service. Again, you're adopting the team and partnership approach. You need to be the one who sets the level of expectation. You want him to view you, your product and your company as the standard to which he compares everything else.

If he responds to the **"IF"** question with a "no," you should go right back at him with a **"WHY"** question to determine what the objection is that is in your way. Then you may want to ask, **"What would I have to do to get your business?"** This question is so basic, yet many salespeople have a great deal of difficulty in asking it. You can even ask him, "What information would **you** need in order to make an intelligent buying decision today?"

Don't be afraid to get to the bottom line very quickly. If you have enough information about his goals, objectives, needs and wants, you can use the "IF" questions to your advantage.

Here's an example of making a call and qualifying the prospect. People are always throwing smoke screens at you. The last thing you want to have happen to you is to be blown off by someone who just doesn't want to take the time to listen to you after you have taken the time to call him on the phone or stop in and see him.

89

Model Scenario: Qualifying the Prospect

Let's say you are selling some type of information system or service, and the prospect tells you that he doesn't need your product or service. It's time for the **"WHY"** question, which you can use for virtually any product or service.

Salesperson: "Why do you feel like you don't have a need for my product?"

Prospect: They give a response.

Salesperson: "Do you have the control over your business that you would like to have?"

Prospect: "No." (This is almost always the answer.)

Salesperson: "If you could hire someone to sit outside your office every day, and every time you asked him a question about your business, he would give you an immediate correct and accurate answer, what would you pay that person?"

Prospect: "A lot." (This is the common answer.)

Salesperson: "How much? Give me a ballpark number."

Prospect: "I can't put a price on it. It would be invaluable."

Salesperson: "Then you would at least pay him minimum wage?"

Prospect: "Oh, absolutely!"

Salesperson: "That's the kind of investment I am talking about here today. For about the cost of a minimum-wage person, I can provide you with a system that will give you the information you need to gain the control of your business that you would like to have. Not only that, the system won't call in sick, won't talk back to you, doesn't require a vacation and won't go on strike. What more could you ask for? And furthermore, it will work nights, weekends and holidays if necessary and never complain or ask for a raise."

Prospect: "That is most interesting."

Salesperson: "Isn't that the kind of support you want and need in your business?"

Prospect: "Sure, doesn't everyone?"

Salesperson: "Then let's take a few minutes to determine exactly what kind of return you could expect on such a small investment."

Let's take the same situation and use a cellular phone as the product to show you that the product or service does not matter. It is the technique.

Salesperson: "Why do you feel that you do not have a need for a cellular phone?"

Prospect: "I have gotten along without one for years and they are too expensive."

Salesperson: "Do you spend a lot of time in your car?"

Prospect: "Yes, about two hours per day."

Salesperson: "Are you accessible any time one of your customers needs to talk to you?"

Prospect: "No."

Salesperson: "Do you think you lose customers as a result of them not being able to get in contact with you, or at least make some of them mad on occasion as a result of being unavailable and non-responsive?"

Prospect: "Probably so."

Salesperson: "If you had an extra two hours a day to telemarket or return calls, how much additional business do you think you could sell?"

Prospect: "Several thousand dollars per month."

Next, have the prospect quantify the additional sales dollars and associated commission or profit dollars, so you can compare that against the cost of your cellular phone and approximated monthly charges. (We will assume the profit exceeds the cost of the cellular phone.)

Salesperson: "Then it appears that you, in fact, could use a cellular phone, and with the additional sales, it wouldn't really cost you anything, would it?"

Prospect: "You are exactly right. When can you install the phone?"

If you've been thinking about what we've covered earlier, you've probably already realized that you have gained his attention by pointing out the potential benefits. In both of the above examples, not only did you qualify your opportunity, but you also created an opportunity that didn't previously appear to exist. You did this by using a line of questioning that built his interest as your line of questioning unfolded.

At this point, the ball is now in your court to prove that you can do what you just told him you could do. If he's not ready to buy at this point, you have at least turned what at first appeared to be a lost opportunity into a qualified prospect. Your next step is to seek his commitment to acquire your product or service by practicing these simple techniques:

- Being honest

- Asking open-ended questions

- Listening carefully

- Then following up with **"If"** or **"Why"**

You will soon become skilled at drawing out objections so you can go for the payoff: **The Close**.

As you become more experienced, you will become more eager to qualify quickly and increase your productivity. The next few chapters outline the techniques of quickly overcoming objections and moving quickly to the close. They also provide you with a handy quick-reference guide to the lifelong rules of the selling game.

The Dynamics of the Sales Call

Selling is no different from the examples above. Selling is what you have been doing all of your life. You meet someone, you establish rapport, you qualify and you go for the close. Why make selling more complicated than it really is?

Let's expand on the "Dating Game" scenario. Although selling and this scenario may not be exactly the same, the dynamics are parallel.

It could be either a girl meeting a guy or a guy meeting a girl. It might go something like this: Guy meets girl and introduces himself. He is trying to establish some type of rapport. He starts talking to her, asking questions on a broad range of topics until he finds an area of common interest. His role at this point is to show interest and understanding. Once she feels that he is in tune with her interests and ideas, she begins to feel more comfortable with him and usually the conversation continues to expand into other areas. The whole idea up to this point is to let her get to know him and start feeling comfortable with him as a person.

At this point, rapport is being established and hopefully will continue to grow. Then the conversation may become more personal than global. They may explore personal likes and dislikes and become more emotionally involved in the topic of conversation in which mutual interest has surfaced.

Let's say his objective is to get a date with her. Once he feels things are moving along smoothly and the timing is right, he will move in for the close. He will probably be looking for a signal to decide when the time is right to pose the question to her. It may be when she says, "I would like to do that sometime." It could be a physical gesture such as touching his arm or hand. Or it could be a certain look in the eye or expression on her face.

Let's say he gets the signal and immediately asks her for a date. She says, "No!" As I said before, at this point he can say, "Hey, I have had enough of this excitement." He can then turn around and leave, or he can hang in there and find out why. It is entirely his decision. Let's say he decides to find out why, and she tells him that she has a boyfriend.

Boyfriend = Brand Loyalty

At this point, Prince Charming has two options: accept the boyfriend as a valid obstacle and move on, or ask more questions about the boyfriend.

• **Seeking Weakness.** He may, for example, try to find out what is so great about this guy or if there is anything she doesn't like about him, subtly, of course. At this point, she may tell him to get lost or she just might respond to his questions. If she is responsive, he might even try to dig a little deeper to find out how serious their relationship is. He is trying to find a weakness. This is no different than calling on a prospect who already has a relationship with one of your competitors.

If he finds a weakness, he may try to capitalize on it and point out that her boyfriend's weakness is an area of strength for him. It also might be a good idea at this point to find out how big the boyfriend is!

Maybe she hates it because her boyfriend does not like to go out on weekends, and a weekend has just begun. Our friend then begins to tell her about a great new restaurant in the neighborhood and how much he would like to have her join him for dinner some Friday night. She responds favorably. He then asks, "What is wrong with right now?"

- **Immediacy.** The challenge is to make something happen **right now** because if he doesn't, he may never see her again. Even if he does see her again, she may not be as receptive. **This might be the only opportunity to make something happen.** She had a slight dislike about her boyfriend, and he is trying to capitalize on it.

- **Objections.** So now, he goes again for the close. But she tells him that she cannot leave because she is with a friend and can't leave her behind. Again, he can give up or hang in there. It is his choice. So he suggests that all three of them go to dinner. She declines.

- **Fallback and Compromise.** At this point he is not losing, but he isn't making progress, either. He decides that she is worth the effort and he is going to continue the pursuit. He can now give her a choice of options. If she really wants to go to dinner, which would be better for her, tomorrow or the next day? He asks, and she commits to tomorrow night. He now has a commitment. His objective was to get a date, but there were obstacles. He could have given up, but he decided the opportunity was there and worth pursuing. Tenacity and persistence paid off, and the fear of rejection was not paralyzing.

Summary

Too often, we make a sales call **more complex** than it needs to be. By asking questions, you can better qualify the real concern and identify the real objections or obstacles. Once you understand the objections or obstacles, you can plan your strategy. In fact, you can **target** your strategy because you know exactly what you have to do. What may at first have appeared to be a real obstacle is now just a minor objection that hopefully can be overcome.

In Part 2, you will learn the specific creative techniques and approaches for handling objections and resolving problems.

PART 2

OBJECTION OVERRULED

CHAPTER 7

GETTING TO "NO"

Qualifying your prospect and getting them to a "yes" or "no" as quickly as possible is critical to your productivity in sales. If a prospect tells you he isn't going to buy from you, that is by far a better answer than a "maybe." You can and will waste hours of your time dealing with "maybe." You want the prospect to tell you very quickly if he will or will not buy from you. You don't need a **"maybe."** You need a "yes" or "no." If you get a "maybe," walk away quickly! "Maybe" is the worst answer you can possibly get out of the three.

Again, by asking the tough questions up front, you can save yourself a lot of wasted time trying to sell someone who has absolutely no intention of doing business with you. Try to anticipate his probable response and known or common objections before they occur. Because no sales situation is completely predictable, you will need to draw out objections in some situations in order to clearly understand what to do next. You should prepare yourself by learning a few key techniques so you won't be thrown by the unexpected.

Learning to Like Objections

Do you like objections? Most people don't. After completing this book, hopefully, you will welcome objections. You will realize that the more effective you become in handling objections, the closer you will come to getting an order. The best way to draw out objections is to **ask people to buy something**. They will start throwing out every type of objection you could imagine and more. That is precisely what you want them to do.

Here are a few fundamental questions people often ask about objections:

- What is an objection?

- Why do people object?

- When will an objection come up?

- What types of objections are there?

- What type of objection is the hardest to deal with?

- How do you effectively handle them?

What is an Objection?

An objection is an argument or opinion presented in opposition to what someone has to say. It is a general feeling of disapproval. Many of the objections you will hear are self-created or hearsay that have very little validity to the issue as hand. Many times objections are thrown out just to blow you off or as an escape ploy to keep you from pinning the prospect down to a buying decision.

It is extremely important for you to understand one thing: **Every objection is an opportunity to close**! The close is when you gain commitment. When a prospect hits you with an objection and you effectively satisfy it, you then have the perfect opportunity to ask for the order.

Guess what happens if he is not ready to commit? Exactly. You will get another objection. It is a cycle. When you get one objection resolved, often another objection will follow. This cycle could go on for a long period of time. However, that is perfectly all right. At least you know what he is thinking. You can flat out ask, "What is standing in the way of you doing business with me?" Then ask, "If it weren't for these three issues, would you do business with me today?" **You want to draw out all of the issues and put**

them openly on the table. Only by asking this question can you truly determine what obstacles stand in the way of a sale.

Again, once you resolve or satisfy the objection, go right back for the trial close and again, ask for a commitment. If he isn't ready to buy, he will let you know and you can start the cycle all over again.

If this type of cat-and-mouse activity appears as though it could go on forever, that is okay. You are developing a more informed buyer. The better informed he is when he makes the commitment, the more sound the order will be. And you will almost always have a more satisfied customer.

The Real and the Unreal

As we've discussed, many of the **obstacles** you will encounter are **self-created**, attitudinal obstacles that you or your prospect bring to the situation. Many other obstacles, however, are just **smoke screens** or excuses the prospect uses to get rid of you. You need to ask a lot of questions to determine if the objection is as it appears on the surface or if there is something else behind the objection. Objections are not problems – they are **opportunities**. That is the fun of dealing with objections. Your ability to resolve objections for prospects shows them you are knowledgeable and there to help. Now that you understand the techniques of questioning and qualifying, let's examine effective techniques for uncovering objections and learning how to handle them.

Basically, there are two types of objections, **REAL** and **UNREAL**. An objection will most likely be real **only** if you allow it to be real because:

THE ONLY REAL OBJECTION IS WHEN YOUR PRODUCT OR SERVICE SIMPLY CANNOT FULFILL THE CUSTOMER'S REQUIREMENT.

Anything else is fair game for you to overcome. By that I mean, if we do not know our business and our products, then it is easy for a prospect to convince us that his reason for not buying is logical and sound. We may accept his objection as real, and give up.

In fact, had we known our product and the competitive product better, we might have been able to show that our product **was** better. Our product could actually be **less** expensive than the competition's and not more, when looking at **actual** cost instead of price.

As an example, if a prospect says she doesn't feel like she needs your product and it costs too much, you can respond with, **"If you felt like you had a need for my product and it was cost-justified, would you buy it today?"** If the answer is yes, then the prospect has just qualified herself. You now know that you have to sell her on the need and justify the product until she feels like it pays for itself.

If she responds with a no, ask her, **"WHY NOT?"** With that question, you should gain a better understanding of why she is not interested in buying the product. If you don't get a good answer, continue to probe the response by asking more questions.

That type of questioning will usually bring out more objections. As a salesperson, that is what you want. Never avoid objections. Try to anticipate the objection in advance and have a comeback ready. Once you get shot down enough, you will begin to figure out what responses work best for your style of selling. Pretty soon you will feel bulletproof and eager to take on the challenge of a new objection that you have never heard.

The smart salesperson knows that most objections are of the second **type**, the **UNREAL**, including all the smoke screens or stalls.

Major and Minor Objections

Whether the objection is real or unreal, it will be perceived by the prospect as being either a major or minor issue.

So here's an inside tip based on years of experience: When addressing these hurdles, **start with and satisfy the minor**

objection first. If you do this, you will find that it is then much easier to overcome the major objections when you get to them. Don't panic if some objections cannot be answered or overcome right away. If your product can satisfy 90 percent of the need, then the prospect is probably far better off than he would have been without your product or service.

Look for your niche of opportunity when confronted with objections. **You do not always have to satisfy every requirement to become the selected vendor.** Sometimes you may only obtain part of the business, but that is better than nothing at all. Once you "get your foot in the door," you are in a position to start building other opportunities.

One percent of something is better than 100 percent of nothing! Be happy if you can just coexist with your competitor in some cases. If your product or service proves as worthy or more worthy than your competition's, I guarantee you that your market share of that particular piece of the business will increase and continue to grow.

It is often unbelievable what opportunity is out there if you only go after it and deal effectively with the objections. All you have to do is remember two things:

1. **THE ONLY REAL OBJECTION IS WHEN YOUR PRODUCT WILL NOT FULFILL THE REQUIREMENT.**

2. **SELLING DOESN'T BEGIN UNTIL SOMEONE SAYS "NO," OR GIVES YOU AN OBJECTION.**

Most of the time, you will just need to know how to handle the smoke screens.

Getting Customers to Sell Themselves

Before we get into specifics, let's look at the general dynamics of objection handling. For example, when people tell you that they don't have a need for your product, you can turn that comment right back and let them **set themselves** up for the buy by showing you the need. The conversation might go something like this:

Salesperson: "Let me ask you, if I were to give you my product today for free, would you take it?"

Prospect: "Sure."

Salesperson: "What would you do with it?"

Prospect: "I would probably _____."

Salesperson: "Why would you want to do that?"

Once he explains how and why he would use the product in a particular area, you can then reply: "It appears to me that you **do** see a potential need for my product, based on what you just told me. Would you like to take a few minutes to see if my product could be cost-justified and pay for itself?"

"If it could pay for itself, then in essence you would be getting it free, wouldn't you? In fact, if the benefit exceeds the cost, it would be like getting the product free **and** a check, wouldn't it? Where else could you find someone who would pay you to take his product?"

Let's look at another example, using office furniture as the product:

Salesperson: "If I were to give you a free ergonomic office chair, would you take it?"

Prospect: "Sure."

Salesperson: "What would you do with it?"

Prospect: "I would replace one of my old, worn-out and uncomfortable chairs with it."

Salesperson: "Why would you do that?"

Again, once he explained why he would use it in a particular area, you could say something like this:

Salesperson: "Wouldn't it be nice to replace **all** of your old worn-out and uncomfortable chairs with new ergonomic office chairs? Can you imagine how happy your employees would be to have comfortable chairs to sit in for eight hours? Do you think that if they were more comfortable at their desks, they might be more productive?"

If the answer is yes, you should try to get him to put a dollar value to it and see if the productivity increase will offset the cost of the chairs. In certain cases, the company image is also more important than the expense, especially when it keeps employee morale at a high level. It may even cut down on absenteeism. You can certainly place a dollar value on that. You may need to probe other areas of concern, such as overtime, versatility, etc.

Questioning such as this draws out issues so the prospects help sell themselves. You can then deal with any specifics that might be standing in the way of getting their business today.

Using Surprise to Reverse the Field

The element of surprise also can help you overcome objections. Occasionally, someone might tell you that he can't buy your product because he is going out of business. That may appear to be a very real objection to many of you. However, what if you turn that situation around positively and ask, "What if my product or service could help you go out of business more profitably?"

You may laugh. However, what does a company do when it goes out of business? It liquidates and pays off its creditors. Whatever monies are left after satisfying its debt are its to keep.

How can a company afford to buy a new product or service if it is going out of business? It's easy. What most companies do when they liquidate is advertise and promote their liquidation. They mark down the price of inventory until it is gone. If they can be more effective in their advertising and promotions, reduce their markdowns a few percentage points and track the fast movers and slow movers, it is possible to save hundreds, thousands or even millions of dollars. It all depends on their inventory levels.

As an example, let's say I had a two-million-dollar inventory and total markdowns equaled 45 percent when liquidation was complete. At that rate, I lost potential revenue off retail of $900,000. Let's say that by controlling markdowns I could liquidate with markdowns equaling 40 percent overall, instead of 45 percent. At 40 percent, I would have lost $800,000 and not $900,000. The savings in markdowns would be $100,000. Not bad if the product or service was less than $100,000.

Your objective is to help the prospect leave the business with more money in his pocket. It can work, and as a result, you still make the sale. That is what selling is all about. Taking an objection and turning it into a sale!

Questions and objections are **sweet words of inspiration** to a professional salesperson. The more information a prospect has, the better his position to make an intelligent buying decision. The better you address or resolve an objection, the closer you are to getting the order. Every sale needs a well-informed buyer. That is why it is good to ask the prospect point-blank, "What information do you need in order to make a decision?"

Countering Negative Associations with Your Product or Service

"Bad press" can cause you a lot of grief as a salesperson. Often, prospects **victimize themselves** with false assumptions or misunderstandings about you, your company or your product. Maybe the prospect has heard that your product did not work for someone else or that it has a short life cycle. As a result, the prospect has no interest in talking to you, let alone buying your product or service.

When this situation occurs, you need to very effectively question him for a better understanding of why he feels the way he does. Maybe your product did not work somewhere else because it was mismatched to the need or was not properly maintained. Had the other person taken better care of the product, it may have lived up to the manufacturer's claim. There could be any number of reasons.

You might respond by saying something like, "Do you consider **your** company to be a good company that is responsive and reputable? Do you consider your products to be quality products?" After a response to these questions, you might ask, "Do you have any dissatisfied customers?" Any company that has been in business for any time at all will have at least one.

Then you can ask him, "Are all of your customer complaints valid, or are some of them invalid and taken completely out of context? What if I spoke to a customer who was bad mouthing you? I could get the wrong idea about you, your company and your product, couldn't I? Especially if I hadn't heard both sides of the story."

Overcome resistance by putting the situation in a perspective to which the prospect can relate. Reverse roles. Question and qualify his objection so that you fully understand where your prospect is coming from and are able to properly relate back to him.

Playing Off Features and Cost

There may be times when your prospect tells you that your product doesn't offer all the functions, features or benefits that your competitor's product offers. When this happens, immediately qualify the prospect to see if he really needs all of those functions or features. If not, then your product may be the better offering, especially if the additional features add to the cost.

Let's say your prospect is looking to buy a pickup truck. Your competitor's truck has four-wheel drive and a sun roof. They are also offering a factory rebate. Your truck offers neither of these options or the rebate. The prices for both trucks are close, but yours is a little less. Which one should the person buy? Obviously, it depends on several factors. However, if the prospect does not need four-wheel drive and a sun roof, who cares about the rebate? Why would he buy your competitor's truck? Even with the rebate, your truck costs less.

If the prospect doesn't need the other features, what may appear to be a bargain on the surface may turn out not to be such a good deal. Salespeople and consumers alike need to look beyond the surface on offers that appear too good to be true. Usually they are – or there are the ubiquitous fine print and unreasonable conditions that must be met. People often get lured into buying because of sales hype or "bells and whistles," when none of these items has anything to do with their real requirements. It is your job as a sales professional to help pull the situation back into focus for them.

In the next chapter, I will address many other issues surrounding objections. At the end of that chapter, you will feel more comfortable in effectively dealing with objections. With practice, you'll soon find yourself very much at ease in asking for the order.

Price vs. Cost

Price is a common objection for all salespeople. Because dollars are the issue, it is important to understand the **difference between price and cost** when ferreting out the real objection. For example, your product may have a higher price tag, but because of the material or construction, it may offer a longer life cycle before replacement is required. It may have a higher residual value, or it may cost less to maintain and operate over time. Residual value is the amount of money your product is worth for resell.

Price is the amount stated on the price tag and the amount you write the check for today. **Cost** is the total accumulation of all the checks you write over a period of time to own the product. Too many times, prospects get swayed into making a buying decision based on price alone and they end up spending more over the long haul because they didn't consider operational or maintenance costs.

For example, the price of a new automobile may be $20,000. However, as a result of owning that car, you are going to incur expenses such as auto insurance, licenses, maintenance, repairs, property tax and so forth. All of these add to the total cost of buying the automobile. The price of the car may be $20,000 – but the cost of owning it is far more.

What appear to be real objections, like price, can be overcome if you know your product, your business and your competition. Referring back to the section on relationship selling, you need to know if your prospect is buying a vendor or a product. If it is you the vendor, then price should not be the primary issue for delaying a decision. It is an unreal objection. When your product or service is being compared to other alternatives and your price is higher, you must be able to show the additional value your product or service offers.

Disarming Budgetary Complaints

Another example of an unreal objection that you will often encounter is, "It isn't in the budget." **Never** accept the budget as a reason for not buying.

If you are selling a copier, the prospect may tell you that there isn't any money in the budget to acquire new equipment. However, that company is going to perform the task of reproduction in some manner. Dollars have been set aside to cover its current copying method, whether it is currently being done by some outside copying service or on the old copier. If it is being done outside, you should contrast the cost per copy, convenience, people time and cost, or courier cost to pick up and deliver, etc. If the firm currently has a copier, you may want to compare quality and its direct effect on the company image. You also may want to compare cost per copy based on the operating expenses, etc., of the two machines. Where possible, quantify all processes and steps in terms of dollars and cents. This will help you negate any price issues.

Then focus on how you can **redirect those same dollars** to pay for your product to do the same task. If you can do it for the same amount or less, then not having enough capital for a new copier is no longer an issue.

As another example, imagine you are trying to sell an automated inventory system. Your prospect tells you that he doesn't have any money in the budget for such a system. You ask him, "Are you going to be in business a year from now?" If his answer is yes, then you know he is going to incur certain costs associated with tracking and controlling his inventory. These could be people costs, outside costs, outside servicer costs, carrying costs, documenting and handling costs, or any number of other items. Your job is to isolate those costs and arrive at the estimated dollar amount to maintain inventory with the current method. If your prospect could reduce his inventory level or become more efficient in handling and tracking his inventory, he could reduce the cost of managing it.

Money is already budgeted – it just isn't budgeted for the use of an in-house automated system. Therefore, if you could show that by installing an automated system, he could control inventory for the same amount of money or maybe a little less than he is currently spending, then money in the budget should no longer be an issue, should it? All you are doing is rechanneling the dollars already allocated to do the job using the current method.

In determining a real objection, then, the smart salesperson will realize that the money is usually there. You just have to **redirect the dollars**.

Your Secret Weapon

You never know when an objection will occur. An objection can occur any time and for any reason. Sometimes you may ask yourself, where did that one come from or what prompted that? Who knows, but who cares? You, of all people, as a professional salesperson should care less. Why? Because you know something about the objection that the prospect probably doesn't know. If it isn't the only real objection, then it is a smoke screen, and you have the ability to figure out how to handle it or resolve the problem.

However, when an objection surfaces, you must stop and address the concern. Always try to satisfy each objection before you proceed. If the concern has been resolved and he still hasn't bought, continue probing and selling. Keep in mind that not all objections can be immediately answered or satisfied. If this is the case, tell the prospect that you will seek a resolution and will get back to him as quickly as you can with an answer. **Then make sure you do it!**

CHAPTER 8

HOW TO HANDLE OBJECTIONS EFFECTIVELY

It's a Way of Life

You will hear all types of objections while you are out there selling. **Listening** to and for objections is a **way of life** for a salesperson. Many prospects think you are just trying to get their money, and they want to hang on to it. This is why you always want to **present your product** as an **INVESTMENT** whenever possible.

The professional salesperson knows that the better he can present his product as an investment, not an expense, the better his odds of closing the order. The more effective he can handle an objection, the closer he is to getting a commitment. I use the term "investment" versus "spend" because investment implies that you will eventually gain a return of some sort on the money. Spend means a cost to you, or an expense. It can have a negative connotation. Most people like to feel that they are getting something of value for their money when they spend, rather than getting nothing.

Overcoming the Natural Resistance to Change

Once you understand that people buy because of some need or want, you also need to realize that **most people resist change**. If your product or service changes the way someone is used to doing things, you may have a major hurdle to overcome before you convince him to buy your product.

Once people settle in, accept and learn how something is done, they usually do not want to go through the process of learning something new. This may come about because of fear of not being able to adjust or adapt to a new way of doing things. It may be fear of the unknown. Maybe they are content with what they have.

As a salesperson, you can deal with this obstacle by showing the prospect how the product or change will enhance his job, improve quality, lower cost or make life easier for him. In your presentation, you should soften the impact of making a change to your product. Convince your prospect that it will be easy to implement, easy to use, and whatever else that might make it a benefit for him.

If you find a company that is happy with the way things are, I will show you a company destined to go out of business. Why? Because the competition will eat them alive. Ask them if they run their business today the same way they did five years ago, two years ago, one year ago or even last month. Their answer should tell you something about their attitude of doing business and receptivity to new ideas. Maybe your product or service can get them back in the race or help keep them ahead of the competition. Companies that are growing are always changing. Just like a family changes when a new addition is added to the household, today you function one way. Tomorrow, you may have to adjust and change your habits.

Overcoming resistance is like putting together a puzzle. You put the puzzle together one piece at a time, and you overcome resistance by resolving concerns one at a time.

Understanding Your Prospect

As an example, let's imagine that your prospect says your product is too expensive. You may take that to mean that your prospect **personally** believes that your product is too expensive. However, what he may have been really saying is that his company never spends above a certain amount for your type of product. In the back of his mind, he may be thinking that if he were to purchase your product, he would have to obtain several sign-offs. The person may be very busy and may not want to go through all the hassle or red tape just to do business with you.

If you address the objection from a personal point of view and it is really coming from the corporate point of view, you are probably going to have to deliver your response a little differently.

Another way to understand what the prospect is really saying is demonstrated in the example of buying a new car. Let's say I am a Mercedes Benz salesperson. You may have wanted to buy a Mercedes for a long time, but you can not afford one.

If I were to ask you, "Would you like to buy a new Mercedes today?", you might say, "No, it costs too much." As a result, I could very easily walk away and lose the sale.

Here's where qualifying can make the difference. I ask if you currently own a car. If you do, I ask if you are currently making monthly payments. If the answer to both of these questions is yes, I might ask, "If I could put you in a new Mercedes today for the same monthly payment, would you buy one today?"

If your answer is yes, then the real reason for not buying a Mercedes isn't that a Mercedes costs too much, **it is the impact on your cash flow**! Learn to keenly question a prospect to get to the root of his objection, so that you can properly address the **real** issue and resolve the **real** problem instead of trying to deal with a smoke screen or false objection. If you don't, you can lose a sale.

In the prior example, from the salesman's point of view, you may have been a suspect for a long time. Today you are a buyer!

As a result of not fully understanding the real issues, you might find yourself making statements that puts your prospect on the defensive. Once you put your prospect on the defensive, you have immediately positioned yourself for an uphill battle.

Of course, when dealing with prospects, you have to know when to cut bait or fish and when to move on to someone else. Only you can determine that. You also have to know when to continue to feed and nurture them, and when it is time to move in for the kill and ask them for their business. I guarantee you, that if you viewed some of your prospects as an outsider, and someone else was calling on them, you would tell him to forget that prospect and move on.

Practice Counts

Being able to respond effectively to objections should become as natural as breathing. The best and quickest way to reach this level of confidence is to make a lot of calls and constantly put yourself in front of potential prospects. Learn from your mistakes. That is where the real skill is derived. The more you get shot down the better you can become. It won't take you long to figure out what doesn't work for you. If you want to try a new technique or response to an objection, first try it on one of your peers, or someone who you know will never buy anything from you. Experiment on someone who can't hurt you.

I used to make practice calls on gas stations just to enhance my techniques and skills, and I didn't even have a product to sell them. It gave me an opportunity to practice where I couldn't get hurt if the approach didn't work.

Be patient. Understand that it may take you awhile to know enough about your product or service to have a high degree of confidence and feel comfortable with what you are doing. **There is no substitute for experience.** In most outside selling jobs, it is hard to sell anything hiding behind a desk in the office where the atmosphere is warm and cozy. Arm yourself with the best defensive coat of armor you can. That coat of armor is your knowledge about your prospect, product and competition. Engage your prospects head-on. "Psych yourself up" to be confident, strong, creative, bold, tenacious, self-motivated and courageous. Then go forward and be ready for anything. **Expect the unexpected!**

If you ask for the order enough times, you will soon find that the objections you get are the same ones over and over all the time, only phrased differently. Once you hit this point in your career, you will be well on your way to becoming more successful. You will have had several opportunities to address a particular objection from a number of different angles. And you will now know which of **your responses** seems to satisfy the objection best. You will see this unfold throughout the book, but to really be good at sales, you have to practice every single day. You need to constantly do a self-assessment of where you are doing well and where you need to improve. Then you need to work on improving both areas.

Winning the Game

Once you attain this level of confidence, you will have achieved the attitude of "Give me your best shot. Give me an objection that I haven't heard before." You don't necessarily have to project this attitude to your prospect, but it can be an uplifting and driving force of motivation for you when you have a high level of confidence. That's when the world of sales becomes fun and exciting. Take each situation as though it is a personal challenge. Then rejoice and recognize the fact that you have met the challenge when the transaction ends up where everyone wins.

As I've said before, selling is often like a game of chess – both buyer and seller are making moves and counter-moves, advances and retreats. Both players are setting up their defenses and their offenses. The buyer is usually trying to negotiate the best deal for himself and the salesperson is trying not to give away the ship, especially if his commission is tied to the profit of the sale.

The question is "Who is in a better position and has control?" In the game of chess, or any sport, the intent is to have only one winner. In business, it should be a win-win situation for everyone involved in the transaction. A **win-win** deal keeps everyone happy and customer satisfaction at a maximum. Some people believe winning is everything. However, in my opinion, for a salesperson, winning isn't everything, but **wanting to win is**!

You may hear thousands of different objections, but once you dissect them, their underlying theme will most likely fall under one of the 16 types that we are going to cover later in this chapter. They also will fall into one of four categories. Once you understand that these types are really smoke screens and learn an effective response, you will find that your close rate will be much greater.

I do not mean to imply that if you memorize the 16 responses, you will be able to conquer any objection you may get. Every objection can have a twist. But these 16 types will give you a solid foundation so you can more effectively address each issue. Study them. Think about them. Then decide how you can use them. In handling objections, always try to respond with a little more information than your prospect expects. It will lend you credibility. That will often set you apart from your competition.

Get Creative

As you read through the 16 types of objections, along with the previous examples I have used, and then later review the 12 closing techniques, you may think I am trying to out-wit or manipulate the prospect. You may even smell a bit of arrogance in the air. If you do, you are mistaken. That is not the intent.

It is okay to be self-confident and even a little cocky, but never manipulative or arrogant. Your customers are your livelihood and future revenue stream. One of them may be the very one who pays for your next toy.

Being creative means saying something profound enough to get your prospect's attention. Once you have his attention, you can begin the selling process. Somewhere during that process you are most likely going to get an objection. When this happens, you need to resolve that objection. If it takes a profound line of questioning, then that is what you need to do. Your job is to keep things in their proper perspective. Keep it simple to understand. Sometimes the most bizarre questions, illustrations or analogies can do that. It often can lighten up things and change the entire tone of the meeting. Yes, it can even abruptly end a meeting, if you don't know what you are doing or you don't know the personality type of the individual. But if you have self-confidence and know who you are and what you are doing, you can effectively get away with a lot of things and still keep the call at a professional level.

It is very important that you understand this. When selling new business, more people will reject your offering than take advantage of it, for any number of reasons. Therefore, when someone tells you he has no interest in your product, you have to get even more creative. After all, the only way you can possibly go is up. So why not try something different? What do you have to lose? He has already told you he isn't going to buy from you.

You certainly don't want to anger, alienate or make enemies, but you will amaze yourself with how many people will respond to something bold, risky, personal or just plain challenging. However, here is a fact. If you don't try something creative to get their attention, you are definitely leaving empty-handed.

Even if you don't get the order, they will at least remember you. That is half the battle right there – getting your prospects to remember you out of all the other salespeople they meet.

I use to sell in a lower economic area where many people criticized me for driving a Mercedes. Many times the prospect would make comments about my car. I would simply reply, "My customers bought me this car out of their appreciation for all that I have done for them. In fact, that is why I am here today. I am here to see when you are going to start contributing your fair share to the monthly payment." Now, I know many of you are thinking, what a "wise guy." However, I can tell you one thing: Not only did it lighten up the conversation, it usually got the meeting and the relationship off to a fast start. In fact, the normal reaction from the prospect was, "Well, you must be doing something right for someone or you certainly wouldn't be driving that type of car. How do you think you can help me?"

When I am selling, I care, but just not **that** much. I **don't take rejection personally** because I know everyone isn't going to buy from me. I can assure you that I am going to get the business if it is at all possible. At least I will have fun trying new, creative ideas to get the prospects' attention and get their business. A new account sales-person, in particular, should constantly be thinking "outside the square." Selling is a job that requires the use of a lot of different strategies and tactics.

I will illustrate what I mean by thinking outside the square by using the following illustration. Without lifting your pen, connect all of the dots in the square using only four lines.

Illustration 3

• • •

• • •

• • •

If you completed this exercise successfully, **CONGRATULA-TIONS!** Otherwise, look under Appendix D for the answer.

Now, let's look at the 16 different types of smoke screens (objec-tions) that you are going to encounter.

THE 16 MAJOR SMOKE SCREENS

UNIQUE REQUEST	**SIZE OF COMPANY**
FINANCIAL JUSTIFICATION	**NEGATIVE REFERENCE**
RECIPROCITY	**DELEGATION**
FEASIBILITY	**FEAR OF THE UNKNOWN**
PRIORITY	**STAFF OR RESOURCES**
LACK OF CONFIDENCE	**UNREASONABLE REQUEST**
EDUCATION	**TECHNICAL AND PRODUCT**
POLITICS	**DEFICIENCIES**
COMPETITION	

UNIQUE REQUEST

A unique request is any request that is out of the ordinary to the way your product performs or does business.

Example: "I want your product to be compatible with my existing equipment, process or environment."

This objection could be a real show-stopper if your product cannot be made compatible to work with the prospect's existing equipment. However, this objection is often just a stall tactic or a way to get rid of you. The other benefits your product offer may outweigh the significance of having the ability to interface. When faced with a unique request, you should ask questions that determine just how important that requirement is for making a buying decision. Is the requirement mandatory or just a nice thing to be able to have? The question is this: Could he get along without it?

Ask: "If I could provide that capability, would you buy the product from me?"

If it is a show-stopper, no matter what the request is, then it is your job to see if you can **modify** your product, service or way of doing business to meet the needs of your prospect. You also need to ask yourself if it is worth the time, effort and cost to pursue the change. Only experience (or asking the right people in your company who have the experience and expertise) can help you determine if it is a project worth pursuing. If it isn't, then walk away and find another opportunity. Remember, selling is a numbers game! You won't get them all, no matter how hard you try!

FINANCIAL JUSTIFICATION

Another objection that often arises has to do with having the available funds. However, if you have a good understanding of finance, cash flow and taxes, this objection can often be very easy to handle.

Example: "It costs too much. We don't have the money in the budget. I cannot afford it."

It may be true that your product does carry a high price tag. However, you need to understand where the objection is coming from.

Ask: "It costs too much compared to what?"

If you sell a product that can make a substantial impact on that company, you might suggest to the person that the only numbers he needs to be concerned about are the numbers seven and eleven, as in Chapter 7 and Chapter 11 bankruptcy and reorganization. This may be a good line to use if your product can add to the company's competitiveness, especially if the competition is nibbling away at their market share.

It isn't necessarily the "total line" on the price quote that causes an objection. It is your inability to help your prospect understand the difference between price and cost and what that difference can mean to him.

As I touched on earlier, it is often critical that your prospect understand the difference between price and cost. Price is the amount he writes the check for today, and cost is the total accumulation of all checks written over time to own and maintain the product. You may have to compare current cost to proposed cost, as well as show the tax impact that the acquisition may have on his company if your product is acquired. Not all products will qualify for a tax write-off. Therefore, you need to know if your product qualifies as a business expense or tax write-off for the customer. Tax benefits depend on the product and how it is to be used.

Imagine you can buy my product for $50,000 or a similar product from my competitor for $40,000. Which would you prefer? Based on this information alone, you would most likely choose the less expensive product because it appears to be $10,000 less. However, when you look at the acquisition based on cost, you may find that you will spend less money for the $50,000 product over time than you would have spent on the $40,000 product.

Example: Assuming your prospect is in the 34 percent tax bracket, let's see how that affects the cost of the two products.

	PRODUCT A	PRODUCT B	DIFFERENCE
Price	$50,000	$40,000	$10,000
Corporate Tax Rate of 34 percent ($50,000 x .34)	- 17,000	- 13,600	3,400
After-Tax Cost	$33,000	$26,400	$ 6,600

What appeared to be a $10,000 difference is only a $6,600 difference after you deduct your tax depreciation.

Now let's look at the additional impact of residual value. Residual value is the amount of money you could get by selling the product after you have fully depreciated it off of your books. Let's say Product A has a 25 percent residual value and Product B has a residual value of 10 percent.

	PRODUCT A	PRODUCT B	DIFFERENCE
Residual Value ($50,000 x .25) A ($40,000 x .10) B	$12,500	$ 4,000	$ 8,500
Actual Product Cost	$20,500	$22,400	$ 1,900

After considering residual value, Product A is actually **$1,900 less** than Product B over the useful life of the products. This is a very simple approach to help narrow the gap in price when comparing two products, especially when you are dealing with capital assets. (I haven't gone into cost of money or **interest rates, time**

value of money or **reclaiming residual value**, etc. These numbers are in their simplest form.)

It is also a major attention-getter that you can use on your prospect. Using this approach will allow you to continue to sell to him.

Suppose a person is unemployed and going for a job interview. He really needs to be wearing a suit for the interview that projects the right image for the job, but he neither owns a suit nor has the money to buy one. So he goes to the interview anyway and ends up not getting the position. Had he invested in a suit to project the required image, he might now be gainfully employed. His earnings the first week could have more than paid for the suit. How much did he lose in the long run as a result of not investing in a new suit? Again, we are comparing price versus cost.

Learn to listen when someone says, "It costs too much." What is he really saying?

Does he really think it costs too much based on his value system? If this is the case, would he refuse to purchase it at any price?

Is he saying he could not afford the monthly payment and its effect on his cash flow?

If cash flow wasn't a problem, would he purchase or invest in your product today?

If that is what he is saying and you could work out the payments so he had the ability to meet the monthly obligation, couldn't you probably make the sale?

If your product can cut costs or generate revenue, it may more than offset the monthly investment for your product. However, the ball is in your court to make that happen. You must clearly show how the benefits can be obtained. You may even need to be able to show him how to obtain financing.

Never accept the "it costs too much" objection as real. Often it is a stall. The person does not understand enough about finance and tax effects to realize that your product is an affordable and good investment for him or his company.

Isolate the objection. Ask: "If you were convinced that the product was cost-justified and it paid for itself, would you buy it?"

Once you gain a "yes" commitment, then prove it is less expensive with some of the techniques used above. And you've got a deal!

RECIPROCITY

This often comes about when someone wants some kind of kickback or favor if he buys from you. It's the old squeeze of "What will you do for me, if I do something for you?"

Example: "If I recommend your product, what do I get out of it?" Or, "Your company never buys anything from us and we have lots of products that your company could use. I will buy from you only if your company starts buying from us."

As serious and as real as this type of objection may seem, it can be overcome if properly handled. First, empathize with the prospect and immediately get your conversation on a business level. Point out that you are making a business proposition – the same type of proposition your company would expect from him if he were trying to sell his products to your company.

Then point out that if, in fact, his product was the best offering, your company would probably select them as the vendor of choice. (That is assuming that there is no contractual obligation that would prevent the change of vendors at this time.) That is what you are trying to do in this situation: Present him with the best possible offering out of all of the competitors. If you are the best, then you would expect him to buy from you. If not, then he should buy from someone else.

Ask: "If we were one of your customers, would you buy my product today?"

Then, if he doesn't have a contact at your company, put him in touch with the person who would be responsible for purchasing his products. Offer to introduce him to that person.

Although kickbacks are a common way of doing business for some industries, countries and companies, business decisions need to be based on business issues. Once you step outside the ethical approach to doing business, you can find yourself violating the law and risking a possible felony charge. No single sale is worth that exposure. Keep things above board. You may be surprised how much respect you can gain when you are honest and ethical and live up to it. People like doing business with people they trust.

FEASIBILITY

A feasibility objection arises when the prospect does not feel that he has the ability to take advantage of your offering. He feels that it wouldn't be likely or reasonable to use the product right now.

Example: "I don't think your product is right for a company our size."

The feasibility objection is almost always a smoke screen. When this type of objection occurs, continue questioning the prospect to find out what the **root** objection is. What other issues, if any, is he currently having to deal with that may not make your offering feasible at this time?

This objection actually may stem from any of the other types of objections. If it is a size issue, as in the example above, you might start by asking, "In what size company do you think our product could best be utilized?" You can then structure your response by saying something like, "On the surface you may very well conclude that. However, the majority of our customers are about your size. In fact, we have many happy customers who are much smaller than you in terms of (whatever)."

Again, isolate the objection. Ask: "If you felt the acquisition was feasible at this time, would you buy it?"

PRIORITY

A priority objection usually comes up when someone feels like he needs to be spending his time or money on something more important than your product or service. Often he won't even take the time to understand how your product or service could help him.

Example: "Although I would love to have a new car, there are more important things that I need to be spending my money on right now."

What initially appears to be a major objection may be a minor objection if properly questioned and put in perspective. Maybe there is not enough cash flow to buy a new car. Maybe he has a car that always runs. Maybe he doesn't realize what it is costing him to hang on to his current car. Maybe he doesn't realize the potential problems and costs that may arise as a result of not getting a better car. He may not realize the potential financial impact of keeping the old car.

If he has been having any kind of problem or irritation with the current car and realizes the impact it is having, you could have a prospect. Buying it today may not be a priority, but if he totals his car tonight, whether he has money or not, tomorrow morning, buying a new car will be at the top of his list of priorities.

Otherwise, ask him: "What would it take or what could you or I do to get this project moved up to a higher priority?"

Ask: "If you felt like this investment offered a greater return than some of your other projects, would you move it up in priority and work on obtaining my product rather than one you may currently be considering?"

Don't be discouraged if someone does not buy from you today, because you never know when things will change, and they can change instantly! Continue the contact regularly, maybe every other month, so that when something changes, the relationship will be established and he will call you first.

LACK OF CONFIDENCE

Lack of confidence objections occur when the prospect does not think that either you or he can make the product work the way it should. Maybe he just doesn't believe your product is any good, or he feels he can't get the service or support he needs.

Example: "I don't believe your product will work for us."

Again, this objection will be real if you don't know enough about your prospect's requirements and your product. You must question for a better understanding of why he feels this way. Then you must be able to convince him that your product will meet his needs, either by a demonstration of your product or service, or by having him witness someone using your product or service in the same manner.

You generally are forced to prove something when this type of objection occurs. So build a substantial arsenal of good references to support your product. **References** will help your prospect gain more confidence in your solution. A reference can be anyone who is using or has used your product and is willing to tell others about how good your product is. It can be a customer you sold or one that someone else has sold. Either way, use a good reference to help you validate the quality or benefit your product or service provides.

Then ask your prospect: "If you felt like you could effectively use the product, would you buy it today?"

EDUCATION

Closely related to lack of confidence, this objection may occur when your prospect feels unable to learn how to adequately use your product or that his employees may lack the ability to learn.

Example: "It will require too much effort or will be too time-consuming to train our people to use your product."

This can be a minor issue if your company provides education or training on the product. Empathize, then give examples of others who felt the same way in the past, but who are now very skilled in using the product after proper training. Again, you are right back to reference selling.

You might even ask him who he feels is the most incompetent person in his organization. He doesn't have to give you a name, but ask, "Does someone come to mind?" Once he tells you yes, ask him, "If I could spend a day or whatever time it takes to train that person to effectively use the product, and that person could effectively demonstrate to you his ability to use it, would you then be satisfied that everyone else in the organization could learn how? If so, would you buy it?"

Show that the product is not that difficult to use. There is a risk in taking this approach. However, right now you don't have an order and maybe not even a prospect. You can gain a prospect if you relieve his concern about his staff.

Ask: "If you felt like your employees could be taught to use the product, would you buy it?"

POLITICS

Political objections often surface when you are not selling directly to the decision maker. The prospect usually delegates the responsibility or blames someone else or some outside factor as the reason he cannot commit to you. He usually implies that he would like to do business with you but, for some reason, conditions are not right or others would not approve. Maybe he implies that career-wise it would not be a smart decision on his part to make a commitment just now, because of other internal issues that are going on. Or, he currently has a good business relationship with one of your competitors that he prefers not to disrupt.

This type of objection may come up more often when you are selling big-ticket items.

Example: "Upper management does not feel that the Board of Directors would approve such a proposal at this time."

What an easy out for the prospect if you don't dig deeper into your questioning! Too often, salespeople accept this smoke screen and move on, when in fact, there could have been a real opportunity to close the sale right then and there. They could at least set themselves up to get the order in the near future.

When this type of objection occurs, find out at once why he feels that way. You might ask him, "What types of things **would** the Board consider and approve at this time?" If your prospect really feels there is a need for your offering, he will usually find a way to present it so that the purchase can be made.

To encourage him, you might say, "Let's pretend for a minute that you were to present this to the Board. What approach would you use and why?" The response may trigger something in your mind that may be helpful in carrying out your objective successfully. Getting your prospect **EMOTIONALLY** involved with your product or service has never been so important. See what information you can provide to help build his case, and then strategize how the **two of you** can best present the offering to the Board.

You also may need to know who sits on the Board, their backgrounds and their own personal objectives. The best way to find this out is to personally make a call on each Board member before you make your presentation. Once you understand all of their goals and objectives, tailor your presentation to satisfy each and every one of them so the odds of your winning the business are extremely high.

In political situations, small items could very well apply. Maybe a family member of the company has an attitude problem with the salesperson or the company. Maybe they have had a bad experience with the product or service. It may not be politically smart to go against the wishes of another member of the family.

Use the method politicians use! Get your votes in the bag before the vote takes place. Urge your advocates to help you with those who may not vote in your favor. If you can show them how your product can help them meet their objectives, buying your product may be the politically correct thing to do. You never know until you pursue the opportunity.

Ask: "If politics weren't involved and you could make the choice on your own free will, do you believe that we have the better product offering? If so, would you buy it from me?"

• **Make it a business issue.** A comment you often get with a political objection is: "My friend or relative sells a similar product. If I were to buy it, I would buy it from him because I know I could get a better deal."

Handle this by staging a scenario to which this prospect can easily relate. Let's say you are going to have open-heart surgery. Your father and I are doctors. You don't even like me. You love your dad, and you can get a great deal from him. It may even be free. The only problem is, dad is a pediatrician and not a heart surgeon. True, he is a doctor, but not what you need. The same holds true in business. All products and services aren't the same, so **take the personalities out of it and make it a business issue**. Help your prospect differentiate between what you have to offer versus what your competitor is offering.

• **Fear of reprisal.** How about this one? "My spouse would kill me if I bought this." Again, you need to question more to find out why your prospect feels like he would get killed, and see if you can turn that response into a positive selling opportunity that benefits the spouse. Turn the reason for not buying into the reason for buying!

Example: "If I brought home that video camera, my husband would kill me."

What do you do? Think back to what we discussed earlier about prospects. Try to **paint a picture** to help the prospect understand the benefits of the purchase. Play on the **emotions**. Ask her the most memorable moment about her children or their life. Ask if they have that event on film. If she answers no, ask if they would like to have had it on film so that they could enjoy that moment for years to come. Maybe she answers yes, but she tells you that it is on 16 mm film and not video.

If she feels that 16 mm has some shortcomings, use that as a starting point to sell video. Point out all of the benefits that video has over 16 mm. You might ask if any major event is about to happen in their lives or the life of a family member. If the answer is yes, then let her point out to you the potential value of owning a video camera and use that as a lead in for the close.

Let your prospects **sell themselves** where possible. You may have to sell the benefits of videotape to film or some other media, but again, figure out what it is going to take and what approach works for you.

Your goal is to guide your prospect until the product or service becomes a necessity instead of "nice to have." Accentuate the positive and get him **emotionally** involved. If he is sold, use him as your inside salesperson to market to those who may be opposed to the acquisition. There is nothing better than having an inside salesperson working for you!

Ask: "If we could get your husband's approval, would you take it home with you today?"

COMPETITION

Sometimes the prospect will ask you who your competition is. He may tell you that he wants to look at competitive offerings. When this happens, you can respond by saying, "There are many fine companies that provide the same or similar product." (If, in fact, there are others.) "You are certainly more than welcome to shop around. However, I believe you will find that we offer a quality product at a competitive price, or maybe even the best price. However, as far as I am concerned, **I am the competition**!" When you display that level of confidence, it is sometimes amazing how quickly you can disarm the prospect – and walk away with an order.

Many prospects feel that they will get a much better deal if they can get two or more vendors competing for their business. They often let you know that there are other alternatives from which they can choose. They may just be looking for more information from you so they can make a more intelligent decision later on, or they may just want to reassure themselves that they are getting the best value for their money. However, if you have done the right job in presenting your product or service in a professional manner, they like you and your product satisfies their requirement, they may just go ahead and buy from you without shopping around.

Is it worth their time, energy and effort to shop around somewhere else to try and save a few dollars when you have what they need right now? Many times they could be using your product and enjoying the benefits of your product while they are still looking around for a better deal.

Example: "I can buy the same product from Acme Company for less money."

When someone tells you they can buy a similar product for less money, ask him why he hasn't already bought it! Turn the price issue right back on him whenever it is possible to discreetly do so.

As an example, you might say to a bank president, "Why are the walls in your bank mahogany, oak, marble, walnut, etc., instead of just sheetrock painted white?"

To a manufacturer: "Why is it you have all those numeric control machines in your plant? You can certainly buy regular machine tools for a lot less."

To an executive: "Why is it that you have a custom wooden desk and not one made of metal?" Or, "Why is it I see a Cadillac, Lincoln, Mercedes, BMW, Jaguar, Lexus, etc., parked in your parking space and not a Yugo?"

Then add: "There is nothing around here that indicates to me that anything you do is based solely on price. So why are you quibbling over a few dollars now **to have the best**?" This approach can work if, in fact, your product is the best for what the prospect requires.

Another approach is to challenge the issue of both products **appearing** to be the same. Once you get beneath the surface, you will probably find that the products are not comparable. **Uncovering the difference is the key here!** Question until you know for sure that your product is different.

• **Set your product apart.** Ask the prospect who his biggest competitor is. You might say, "If your competitor said that his product was better than yours, would he be telling the truth?" Most people will defend their own products. Not only will they tell you theirs is much better, but they will also take the time to show you and explain to you why it is better.

Then you simply reverse the situation and ask him, "If your competitor told me his product was better and I could buy it for less, would that be true?" Point out that he is in the same position now that you would be in if that happened. Then add, "However, if you can point out to me the difference between misconception and fact, I might just buy your product rather than his." I might buy the product simply because I took the time to understand the difference between the two.

"That is now what I have to do for you with my product. I have to convince you to take the time to differentiate between my product and my competitor's." Then clearly show where your product warrants the additional cost, if there is one. The difference may be in workmanship, the quality of materials used, additional features, service and support, or maybe it is the type of warranty.

Equate the difference with dollar and cents when possible. Otherwise, it's a "me, too." You may appear to just be selling a commodity that your prospect can get anywhere. If it is a commodity, his buying decision will probably be based on price alone. If you aren't the lowest price, you will probably lose.

Ask: "If you felt like our product was equal to or better than the other product using the same selection criteria, would you do business with me?"

• **Avoid the big switch.** Sometimes people will like your product and get sold quickly on the idea of purchasing it, but they will still want to shop around. After evaluating other vendors, they tell you they are going to acquire it from someone else.

If you work for a large and well-known corporation, you might try this next approach. It may sound strange, but you will be surprised at how many people will respond.

Ask the prospect if he owns any stock in the other company. If he says no, ask him if he owns any stock in **your** company. If the answer is yes, add: "Then help me understand why in the world you would want to invest in a company other than your own?" He might respond, "You are right, let's do it!" As odd as it sounds, it can work if you are dealing with an individual who takes a lot of pride in ownership. It can work especially well if your competitor is a less familiar household name. This is one way that name recognition can work to your advantage. If he doesn't own any stock in either company, you can respond that you were just curious, and move on.

Ask: "Do you own any stock in that company? Do you own any stock in my company?"

SIZE OF COMPANY

This type of objection occurs when the prospect feels that your company is just too big or too small. First, let's look at being too big. Maybe your prospect feels that he would just be a small customer, compared to your other clients. He may feel that if he needed help, your company would not provide the level of support he requires. He may feel you would be committing most of your resources to your larger customers and forget all about him, the little guy. He may feel you would not give him the attention he would like to have. Or perhaps the larger competitors in his own industry are making it difficult for him to compete within his own market, so he is biased against large companies in general.

If he feels your company is too small, it may be because he's concerned about the available resources you would have to support him if he really needed help. He also may be concerned about your experience level, your financial stability or your ability to compete with the big boys.

When you get an objection to your firm's smallness, you might find this approach to be very effective, especially if you are talking to an owner of a larger business. Point out that they were once small and look at them now. You are today where they were some time in the past. People gave them a chance and that is what you are asking for today from them – the same chance. The chance to prove yourself.

• **Familiarity and locale.** Being an outsider can be a real problem if you sell in rural areas or to various ethnic, religious and social groups. They may never tell you why they won't buy from you, but it could very easily be because you are viewed as an outsider and they prefer to support their own people.

Example: "We prefer to buy from a local business rather than from someone located many miles away. You are here today and gone tomorrow. The people around here are here to stay. If we have a problem with something, we can go right to their houses, if necessary. We know them and we know where they live. They are one of us. We try to help each other around here."

The most effective way to handle this is to be empathetic. Acknowledge your understanding of how your prospect feels, then try to take his negative remark and turn it into a positive reason for doing business with you. For example, after you empathize, you might be able to use the size of your company and the depth of your resources to convince him that, in fact, you can provide the same level of service and support as any local business. The size of your company might be a major benefit to them. Not being local then takes on less significance.

The fact that your company isn't physically located nearby also can become a minor issue if he still has the ability to deal with your company directly. Show that he won't be required to go through a middle man, and the support will be equal to or better than the support that he may currently be getting. Emphasize that you are just a phone call away. Maybe your company even has service people or a local representative living in the area.

The sheer size of your company, if it is large, can also help ensure that he is not dealing with a fly-by-night firm that may go out of business at any time.

Ask: "If you felt like you could get the same level of service and support from me that you could get locally – or maybe even better – would you buy the product or service from me?"

NEGATIVE REFERENCE

The negative reference usually comes from someone who does not like your product or has been misinformed about the product, you or your company.

Example: "A friend of mine had your product and he said that it never worked the way he was told it would."

This may very well be true, but it also can be a very minor objection. First, you need to determine who the friend is because you may know the details behind the dissatisfaction.

If you do not know, then question your prospect about why the product didn't work. It could have been because the management commitment was not there to make it work. It could have been because the product was not properly maintained. It could have been because the product was being used in a way for which it was not designed. Maybe it was because of product abuse.

Then point out references who are very satisfied with your product, and give your prospect the names and phone numbers of those people to contact for verification of its quality.

Once the issue is overcome, show how the product could positively work for him and explain what steps you will take to help ensure that he will be totally satisfied.

Ask: "If you felt the product would perform as stated, would you buy it today?"

DELEGATION

Delegation obviously occurs when you are selling to someone who may not have the authority to make the decision, or he does not want to take the responsibility for making the decision. It's an easy out for not buying. This is similar to political objections, except in the political situation, the person is more concerned about what others think than in relinquishing responsibility for the decision.

Example: "I want my accountant or financial officer to review your proposal and if he says okay, then we will do it." Or, "My husband would have to make that decision." Or, "I want Jane to look at this. She knows far more than I do, when it comes to something like this."

This is your signal to determine which of them will really be making the decision. If the other person will be playing the role of recommender and not decision maker, you need to get the commitment from the decision maker that if the other person supports the purchase, then the decision maker will make the commitment to buy the product. Then find out as much as you can about the other person and the criteria he will be using to evaluate the offering.

Let's say you are selling an automatic vegetable-dicing machine to the manager of a restaurant. The manager says he will buy it if the salad chef recommends it. Why is he involving the salad chef? What role will the salad chef play in the decision? What criteria will he be using to evaluate the proposal? You need to know all of these things, because if the dicer will be doing the work that the salad chef normally does, the chef may view the dicer as a means to replace his position. If he takes this view, it is highly unlikely that he will recommend buying it.

Let's look at another example. Let's say you are selling a computer to the president of a company, and he says that he needs to run the proposal by his accountant. "If the accountant says it is okay, I will buy it." Again, why is he involving the accountant? What role is the accountant going to play in the decision? What criteria will he be using to evaluate the proposal? Who is the accountant? What work does he do for the company? Does he have a system installed? What kind? The reason this is important is because it may take revenue away from the accountant, and he certainly does not want to lose revenue. If he has a computer, he will probably recommend the kind he has because he understands it. He also may suggest that they be compatible. If price is a concern, he will probably recommend a Personal Computer, even though the PC may not be the right machine.

In both cases, you need to ask the prospect, "Do you feel that you will get an unbiased decision from this person, or could there possibly be a conflict of interest?"

Ask: "Who is going to be making the final decision?" If he says he is, but he needs reassurance, you might politely ask if he would care to pick up the phone and call that person right now.

Ask: "If the accountant (or whoever) supported the recommendation, would you order the system right now?"

FEAR OF THE UNKNOWN

This objection usually pops up when someone is apprehensive or afraid of taking a chance because he hasn't been exposed to your company or product and knows nothing about what you might be able to do for him.

Example: "I am not certain that your product will work for me."

It may be a fear of not being able to afford or operate the item. It may be a fear of what someone else will say or think if he buys it. Regardless of the type of fear, he will probably try to hide it. You need to isolate it, draw it out and address it until the fear has been eliminated, or at least eased. Letting the prospect see, feel, touch or use the product is one of the best ways to eliminate fear.

This is usually an easy objection to overcome because all you have to do is question to find out exactly how he is doing something now or why he is apprehensive. Empathize, then reference someone like himself who has gone through the same thing and is now a very satisfied customer. If necessary, have him contact the reference. Sometimes a demonstration or a trial period on your product will relieve any fears he may have.

Ask: "If you felt comfortable right now that you could use the product and make it work, would you buy it today?"

STAFF OR RESOURCES

This objection may occur if the person feels that he does not have the qualified staff to get the best use from your product. He may feel that he lacks the manpower because of his current workload or resource commitment to other projects. Maybe he feels that if he acquired your product, he would have to hire someone new, and he doesn't want to staff up at this time.

Example: "I do not have the personnel to implement your product."

This may be a fact. However, if your product can help increase productivity, improve cash flow, reduce operating expenses or increase profits, it may be in the prospect's best interest to staff up anyway. The benefits of having your product may far outweigh the cost of that new employee. You also can suggest that he use a third party or contract with an outside company to come in to set up or install your product. Maybe by the time this is all done, someone on the staff will be freed up to take over its operation. Once someone becomes available, the contract person or new hire could then train others on how to use the product at his convenience and then leave.

Ask: "If you felt that you had the available staff, would you buy the product today?"

UNREASONABLE REQUEST

This type of smoke screen usually requires you or your company to do something that is not feasible or practical from a business point of view. Maybe the request is beyond the scope of service and support your company can provide.

Example: "I will buy your product if you give me a 50 percent discount."

This may be totally unreasonable because of your markup. Your markup may not even be close to that amount. An unreasonable request is a frequent smoke screen, because the person has no intention of doing business with you in the first place. However, he could be fishing for a bargain.

Determine if he is serious or not. Ask very bluntly, "If I were to give you the 50 percent discount, would you give me the order right now?" A question like this will qualify him very quickly. It is either "put up or shut up" time for him. You may even ask, "How much would you be willing to pay?"

Even if you know you cannot meet his request, **still** ask the question. Then turn the question on him and ask what he would do if he were presented with a similar situation by one of **his** customers.

141

Would he do it? Usually when you put the prospect in your position, he realizes that you cannot meet the request. Generally, he will be open to a reasonable compromise if he is a serious buyer.

Ask: "If you were the president of my company, would you do that? Would you consider that a reasonable request?" If they answer no, then ask, "Then why would you expect our president to do anything different?"

TECHNICAL AND PRODUCT DEFICIENCIES

As emphasized earlier, **this is the only real objection that exists**. The only real objection is when your product cannot meet the requirements of the prospect. As you have seen, any other objection can usually be satisfied if properly identified and approached in an appropriate and logical manner.

Example: "Your product does not do what we need it to do."

About the only thing you can do if your product does not have the features or capabilities to do the job is to determine if it would be worth your efforts to pursue the problem. Perhaps your company can either modify the product or develop a product to meet the prospect's requirement.

Ask: "If I could provide that function, would you buy the product from me?"

Be careful. It may not be a realistic request if time is a factor or if the development or modification cost would be prohibitive when compared to the return your company would receive.

It is usually smarter to walk away from this type of situation and find another prospect. They could cost you and your company money in the long run. If you suspect a potential problem in this account, tell your prospect that you would like to be able to help him, but at this time it appears your product doesn't exactly meet his needs.

Then refer him to your competitor. Let your competitor deal with him while you go sell to a **good** prospect. That's one way to keep your competitor off the street and out of your territory!

You will be amazed at how effective this technique can be. If you have been in sales for awhile, can you think of an account that you wished you had never sold because of the problems it caused you and your company? Again, this type of customer can keep your competition tied up so much that they will have little time to call on anyone else. It will for certain keep your competitor off the streets and out of your territory.

Four Major Categories of Objections

All 16 types of objections that we have just discussed can be placed into these four basic categories as follows:

- PERSONAL

- FINANCIAL

- CORPORATE

- TECHNICAL

You don't need to remember the details of all 16 types, but it is important for you to understand that your prospect is usually coming from one of these four points of view. To best respond, you need to be in "sync" with your prospect, or at least on the same wavelength. Here is an easy way to interpret his perspective:

PERSONAL	**ORGANIZATIONAL**
Feasibility	Stall
Priority	Education
Lack of Confidence	Reciprocity
Competition	Delegation
Size of Company	Feasibility
Negative Reference	Priority
Delegation	Politics
Reciprocity	Competition
Fear of Unknown	Size of Company
Stall	Negative Reference
Unreasonable Request	Staff or Resources
Politics	

FINANCIAL	**TECHNICAL**
Financial Justification	Unique Request
Feasibility	Feasibility
Priority	Competition
Competition	Negative Reference
Delegation	Stall
Stall	Unreasonable Request
Unreasonable Request	Technical and Product Deficiencies

READY-REFERENCE RULES FOR HANDLING OBJECTIONS

1. Create a relationship with the prospect. Listen attentively and show interest in what he says. Good eye contact is essential. Pay attention to your facial expressions and voice inflection.

2. Anticipate and try to answer objections in advance. Develop and practice several replies for each type of objection that may occur.

3. Ask questions. You can never ask enough questions. It seems like it is always the question you don't ask that comes back to haunt you. Ask open-ended questions that make your prospect think!

4. Question to draw out objections. **Listen** to and fully understand each objection. Make sure you are on the same wave length as your prospect. **Clarify** his response to ensure you fully understand what he is saying.

5. Verify that you fully understand the question or objection, then address it before you move forward.

6. Avoid the use of the word "I," which makes you the focus rather than the prospect. Keep personalities out of the conversation and the discussion focused on a business level.

7. Don't argue. That puts the prospect on the defensive. If you argue, you usually lose.

8. Avoid "Yes, but..." That puts you on the defensive.

9. Don't guess. If you don't know the answer to a question, admit that you don't know, but tell him you will get back to him as soon as possible with an answer. Write it down so that you do not forget to research for the answer.

10. After effectively handling **each** objection, go for the close.

11. Keep calm, be observant, be alert and remember that an objection is nothing more than an opportunity to close.

PART 3

CASE CLOSED

CHAPTER 9

TIMING AND DELIVERY

NOTE: It may not be necessary to satisfy every objection in order to close the business. Sometimes the purchase may be acceptable even though all issues have not been resolved. This is because there has never been a product designed that was 100 percent perfect.

You must always be prepared to close a prospect if the opportunity presents itself. Closing an order is like a comedian telling a joke. **Timing is everything!** Like timing the punch line for a laugh, you have to time your close at just the right moment if you want a commitment. If you move in too soon or too late, you could blow the whole thing.

The right time is when the prospect's excitement and desire are at a peak and most of the objections or delays have been put to rest. You can usually tell by his positive comments, positive gestures, body language or his ideas for other uses of the product or service.

EVERYTHING YOU SAY and EVERYTHING YOU DO are critical when you are going for the close. All eyes are upon you. If the prospect still feels like you are just trying to sell him something, then you haven't properly done your job. Make certain you relate how the product can be beneficial to him. Again, whenever possible, present your product or service as an **investment** and be able to show clear, tangible benefits. This approach will make the commitment easier to secure.

Your attitude and delivery are also critical when going for the close. Your attitude needs to be positive and your delivery smooth and well prepared. **HAVE YOUR CLOSING REHEARSED,**

REHEARSED, REHEARSED! You need to rehearse your techniques in advance, because your final delivery can make or break your opportunity for the sale. Don't mess it up by not being prepared.

For some salespeople, the close is the most difficult part of the entire selling process because you have to ask someone to do something and you are afraid the answer may be "NO." You can overcome your fear by understanding questions about the close such as these:

- When do you close?

- Where do you close?

- What are the most effective closing techniques?

- Why do salespeople have difficulty in closing?

- Why do prospects have difficulty in making a commitment?

The next two chapters will answer all of your questions. Closing is the natural outcome of the selling process. It is where all of your efforts pay off. It is where the prospect peaks emotionally. It is where you move the prospect over all psychological barriers, to the point of no resistance, to the point of making a firm commitment. Hopefully, the commitment will be a firm order to buy your product or service. However, the commitment does not have to be an order. It can be a commitment to do something positive that moves the selling process forward and will bring the commitment for an order a little closer.

What is the objective of every close?

TO GAIN A CUSTOMER COMMITMENT

When and Where to Close

Closing is the most satisfying part of the selling process, so you want to get there as quickly as possible. It is the one point in the sales process where you can physically see the results of your effort. When do you close? Where do you close? The answer is surprisingly simple:

ANY TIME
ANY PLACE

Get 'em While They're Hot!

You don't want to let a closing opportunity pass you by. You want to close whenever the prospect is **HOT!** You can close at your place, my place, the Board room, restroom or bar room. It makes no difference where it is, as long as someone is ready to buy. Ask for the order! It could be the only opportunity you will have to get it. Your prospect may never be in the mood again if you allow him to leave or give him a chance to cool off.

Can you think of a time when you may have gotten in your car and drove to a store to buy something? Once you got there, you walked out empty-handed because there was no one around to help you. Perhaps the salesperson failed to encourage you to buy the item, so you left the store without buying the product. Don't let anyone walk away without asking him to buy. It is your job as a salesperson to ask him to buy and to see that he does. After all, the revenue from the sale is what pays your salary and commissions.

You May Not Get a Second Chance

In a situation like the one above, have you ever told yourself as you left the store that you were glad that you did not buy the product? You could have been a sound prospect, but you turned into a lost opportunity. Had only the salesperson asked you to buy, maybe you would have left the store with product in hand. Had you purchased the product, you would have rationalized about how glad you were that you bought it. Instead, you rationalized why you were glad you **didn't** buy it. As a result, you may never get in the mood again to make that purchase. That is why I say, **"Get 'em while they are HOT!"** You may not get a second chance!

151

He May Buy from Your Competitor

Worse yet, many prospects go next door and buy from your competitor simply because your competitor asked them to buy and you didn't.

Listen to your prospect's remarks. Read the signs. Watch for anything else that might indicate to you that he is ready to commit.

When in doubt, always try a trial close. If he isn't ready to commit, he will certainly let you know. If you ask why, he will usually tell you that, too. **But you will never know unless you ask for the order.**

The Easiest Way to Get Someone to Buy from You

The easiest way to get someone to buy from you is very simple: **ASK IF HE WOULD LIKE TO BUY!** A good salesperson is not afraid to ask for the order. That is his job. If someone tells you that there is a salesperson here to see you, don't you expect him to ask you to buy something? If he doesn't ask you to buy, aren't you a little surprised? Another question for you to consider is this: Would you want to hire this person to sell for you?

It isn't any different for the prospect that you are calling on. If you are a salesperson, the prospect expects you to ask him to buy something. That's why you carry the title of salesperson. You sell! At least, you **should** be selling.

Getting it Down to a Transaction Basis

Let's take a look at how your delivery can impact the response of the prospect when you ask for the order.

Assume that you are selling a water filter. The average useful life for that filtration system is three years. The last thing you want to do is go in and start selling the water filter at a cost of, say, $200. What you do want to do is to start off something like this:

Salesperson: "Do you ever purchase drinking water from a service or the grocery store?"

Prospect: "Yes."

Salesperson: "How often?"

Prospect: "Weekly."

Salesperson: "How much do you spend per week on bottled water?"

Prospect: "I only spend about $4 per week."

Salesperson: "For a cost of about $.18 per day, you can have the same quality of water in your kitchen sink. If you already spend about $208 per year on water, I could save you about $141 a year if you buy this filter."

Prospect: "You are right. I will take one."

It is much easier to sell $.18 per day than to ask for $200 up front. The $200 up front might immediately turn him off to your product. By getting it to a transaction basis, it becomes a little easier to swallow.

Imagine that you are calling on a pharmacist, and you are going to ask him to buy a computer.

Salesperson: "Do you have the ability to do drug interaction?"

Prospect: "No."

Salesperson: "Would you like to?"

Prospect: "Yes."

Salesperson: "Can you do daily third-party billing?"

Prospect: "No."

Salesperson: "Would you like to?"

Prospect: "Yes."

Salesperson: "Can you give your customers an annual recap of all their pharmacy purchases?"

Prospect: "No."

Salesperson: "Would you like to?"

Prospect: "Yes."

Salesperson: "I can give you all of that for about $50,000."

The pharmacist would probably laugh at you all the way to the door. Instead, by saying: "I can give you all of that for about $.06 per script." He is likely to respond:

Prospect: "Really? I can certainly afford that."

Do you see the difference in how you can state the close? The pharmacist is still going to pay $50,000 for the system, but $.06 per script sounds much more feasible than $50,000. He is accustomed to getting price increases, and $.06 is nothing to him. So think about how to quantify your product or service as part of your delivery. It can make a drastic difference in the result you get from the prospect.

If he is an impulse buyer, you may not have to go through the entire sales process. Again, the way to find out if he is ready to buy without having to go through the entire process is to trial close the business. As an example, ask, "Would you like for us to deliver it, or would you prefer to take it with you?"

To summarize closing the call, first make certain that all of the issues and concerns that can be satisfied have been properly addressed. Make certain that the prospect is emotionally involved and has enough information to make a sound investing decision. Look to see if he is making all the right gestures and comments.

When things look right, **GO FOR IT!** The worst that he can say is no. If this happens, qualify the "no," draw out the objection, satisfy the objection, and again, go for the close.

The Final Step is Key

The final step of the close is the key:

ASK FOR THE ORDER AND THEN
SHUT UP!

The first person who speaks, **LOSES!** It may seem like an eternity, but you have to wait in silence. Let the prospect speak first.

Then be prepared. Closing is a vicious cycle. If he is not ready to buy at this point, you can be assured that another objection will surface. When it does, clarify it, satisfy it and once again go for the close. More objections aren't bad. They show that the prospect is still looking for more information. The more effective you are in addressing his concerns, the closer you are to getting the order.

To help you practice, the next couple of chapters outline helpful tips for the call and suggest closing phrases that should become part of your daily sales vocabulary.

CHAPTER 10

TWELVE CLOSING TECHNIQUES THAT CLINCH THE SALE

Many times, you will have to ask for the order four or five times before you get a commitment to buy. Maybe the rejection came as a result of a premature close or the lack of enough information to make an intelligent decision. When the prospect rejects your first request to buy, you need to come back again with another closing technique. This chapter will give you an arsenal of techniques from which you can choose.

There are many different closing techniques, called by any number of different names, depending upon to whom you talk or what material you read. More techniques have been devised than I will cover here, but these are some of the most useful. If you learn how to use just four or five of these techniques, you will greatly enhance your closing rate. With every new closing technique you master, you increase your odds of success. Understand the techniques and how they can be used, then choose the ones that best match **your** style and personality.

These are the 12 techniques that can add **ZAP** to your ability to gain a customer commitment and close business.

BASIC FUNDAMENTAL CLOSE
SUBORDINATE QUESTION CLOSE
IMPENDING EVENT CLOSE
ALTERNATE CHOICE CLOSE
PUPPY DOG CLOSE
BEN FRANKLIN CLOSE
REFERENCE CLOSE

ASSOCIATION CLOSE
NEGATIVE CLOSE
THINK IT OVER CLOSE
CAN'T AFFORD NOT TO CLOSE
LOST SALE CLOSE

For illustration, let's use a computer as the product example. Everyone today knows what a computer is. It is relatively expensive and can be considered a capital asset, and many other products fit the same scenario.

However, these techniques are certainly not limited to expensive products. They will work for inexpensive products, as well as services. Some of the examples used here will help you save time and make you money as you go for the close. They also may give you some insight into your own future buying decisions.

Today, it is no longer a question of whether or not you can afford a computer. The question is, "Can you afford not to own a computer?" Every company today can afford one. Just how small of an investment will be required is the only issue to be resolved.

That is the question you need to be asking. "Can you afford not to have my product?" Or, "What is it costing you not to have my product?" No matter what the investment, you should give the prospect a good idea of what the return will be as a result of him acquiring your product or service before he spends the first dime.

So get creative and start thinking outside the square. Look at the steps below to figure out how you can use these techniques to help sell **your** products or services.

BASIC FUNDAMENTAL CLOSE

- Make a confident assumptive statement. You know the prospect will buy.

- Summarize the important points in his terms, terms he understands.

- Ask a closing question.

- **SHUT UP.**

For example, "once you install the system" could be the assumptive phrase. You are assuming he is going to buy.

Salesperson:	"Do you agree that you will be able to increase your productivity by 5 percent, which will mean $100,000 per year in increased productivity, or $500,000 over a five-year period."
Prospect:	"Yes."
Salesperson:	"Do you feel that by installing an accounts receivable package, you could reduce your bad debt by 30 percent, which would be worth $6,000 per year, or $30,000 over a five-year period?"
Prospect:	"Yes."
Salesperson:	"And do you agree that you could reduce your inventory level by 10 percent or $100,000 with a 25 percent carrying cost, which would be another $25,000 per year, or $125,000 over the next five years? A total savings in inventory of $225,000 over five years."
Prospect:	"Yes."
Salesperson:	"Then the total benefit and dollar savings you will enjoy is about three-quarters of a million dollars over the next five years."

This is the summary part of the close. It is important here to reiterate all of the dollar benefits. Calculate and expand all of the benefits over the useful life of the product in order to magnify the benefit return. In this case, I chose to expand the amount of three-quarters of a million dollars over a five-year period because it sounds much more impressive than $151,000 per year, or $755,000 over the next five years.

Now for the close ...

Salesperson: "Let's do it!"

THE SUBORDINATE QUESTION CLOSE

- Make it easy for the prospect to say "yes."

- Use an implied major and minor question.

- Then a "yes" to the minor question makes it easier for a "yes" to the major question.

The idea here is to eliminate any negative tone that may keep the prospect from acquiring your product. Your goal as a salesperson is to draw on questions that you know will have a positive or "yes" response. Ask questions that reflect previous minor concerns or objections that already have been resolved and are now satisfied. As he is answering "yes, yes, yes" to those minor issues, it will be easier for him to respond with a "yes" to the major concern, making the commitment to buy easier when you say, "Let's do it!"

Not all decisions are as simple as just doing it. Often, the decision to buy comes after wrestling with many obstacles that could cause the decision not to be made. As the prospect sifts through the maze of hurdles, he finds some of the hurdles to be major and others to be minor as the decision process takes place. Most major decisions are made after a number of smaller obstacles have been resolved. It is the logical thought process.

What you are trying to do is eliminate any negative tone to the decision and create an aura of positives for acquiring your product or doing business with your company. Once he has the rhythm of saying "yes," it becomes easier for him to say "yes" when you ask him to buy.

An example of a subordinate question close may go something like this:

Salesperson: "Do you agree that the proposed system will help you gain a better control of your business?"

Prospect: "Yes."

Salesperson: "Do you agree that your employees will be more productive using the system?"

Prospect: "Yes."

Salesperson: "Do you agree that your employees should be able to easily learn how to use the system effectively?"

Prospect: "Yes."

Salesperson: "And do you agree that the payback more than meets your normal investment criteria of a 36-month payback?"

Prospect: "Yes."

Salesperson: "Then the only decision left to be made is the commitment to invest in the construction of a new computer room, right?

Prospect: "Right."

Salesperson: "With all of the benefits that we have identified, you can construct a new computer room and still exceed your ROI (return on investment) goal. Would you agree?"

Prospect: "Yes."

Salesman: "Then let's do it!"

You can see how all of the minor issues have been resolved, and the only major obstacle is the cost of building a new room. After all of the minor issues have been resolved then it is much easier to address the bigger issue.

IMPENDING EVENT CLOSE

- The prospect has indicated that something has to happen before the commitment will be made.

- A delivery date must be met. A meeting may have to take place. A budget or credit may have to be approved. Maybe a spouse or partner has to give his or her sign-off.

The decision is conditional on the actions of one of the parties before the commitment can become final. Some examples of this might be:

Salesperson: "If I can get your delivery by mid-May, will you place the system on order today?"

Prospect: "Yes."

If he commits, then it is **incumbent upon you** to make it happen by mid-May. If you can, you should walk out with a firm order.

Salesperson: "If I could demonstrate to you how our software meets your specific requirement, would you buy the system from me?"

Prospect: "Yes."

Again, it is your responsibility to demonstrate the fit.

Salesperson: "If the money isn't cut from the budget, will you buy the system from me?"

Prospect: "Yes."

If the answer is yes, then you need to help ensure that the budget for your product isn't cut. One of the best ways to salvage your chances with the budget is to show that the ROI (return on investment) on your product offers a better return than some of the other expenditures being considered. Capital may not even be an issue if you use the avoidable or displaced cost approach. An avoidable cost means a cost that firms won't have to incur down the road. Displaced cost is when they can eliminate some current expenses as a result of having your product. Do some homework on your product, and this method can really work for you!

ALTERNATE CHOICE CLOSE

- Give the prospect only two choices.

- Always start with the words: "Which do you prefer?"

- You win with either answer.

An example of this close might be: "Now that you understand the difference between a typical file-structured machine and the technology that a data base machine offers, which do you prefer for your company?" When he responds, ask for the commitment.

Another closing approach might be to ask, "Which color would you prefer, white or blue?" Then ask for the commitment.

The idea behind this closing technique is to ensure that both choices give you the business. There could be more than two choices, but if you have really done your job in determining their requirements, then two choices may be one too many. Then, if you offer only one solution, you have limited your options. After all, if you offer one option and the prospect says no, then you are out of the competition.

Most of us feel better if we make decisions knowing we have a choice, instead of being boxed in with only one alternative or with someone telling us what we need. If your prospect feels that you have done your job in fully understanding his requirements, and you know your products, he will appreciate having you narrow down the options that best satisfy his needs.

This close is very effective on the aggressive "A type" or "driver" personality. This personality wants to always be in control, be dominant, as well as being results oriented, net and to the point. He usually likes to have a choice because it gives him the feeling of having power and being in control.

THE PUPPY DOG CLOSE

- "The try it – you'll like it" approach.

- Let the prospect use, try or sample your product.

An example of this type of close might go something like this:

Salesperson: "If I allowed you to try the product for 30 days, and it met your expectations and requirements, would I have your commitment to keep the product?"

Prospect: "Yes."

The key to any try-and-buy program is to make **certain** that you and the prospect fully understand exactly what is being evaluated and what criteria he will be using to measure the results of the product. Ensure that someone specifically is assigned the responsibility to **test and measure** the results over a specific time frame. It needs to be understood up front that if the person doing the evaluation agrees that the product met the criteria, then the prospect will keep the product at the end of the evaluation period.

I used this technique many years ago, even before I knew it was a technique. I ran a kennel and bred show stock German shepherds. I had the best guarantee in the business. You had 48 hours to take the puppy to the vet of your choice. If there was anything wrong with the pup, I would pay the vet bill and replace the puppy with another, or take the puppy back and give you a complete refund. If the puppy was sold for show stock, I would guarantee the dog to win at least once if it were shown four times. How many dogs do you think I got back during those five years? **NONE!**

Usually, you sell a puppy at eight weeks old, and they aren't shown until they are about four months old. After the buyer has had a couple of months to become attached to the dog, do you think he would consider sending a puppy back? No way! He would not have sent it back even if it was a "dog." However, you will be pleased to know that every dog I sold and guaranteed to win, did win. My program was not a come-on or fraudulent. You will find that this technique is a great way to get your prospect emotionally involved.

BEN FRANKLIN CLOSE

*   Show the positives versus the negatives.

Ben Franklin would always make a decision after weighing the pros and the cons of the situation. If the pros outweighed the cons, he would go with it. If the cons outweighed the pros, then he wouldn't.

This type of closing technique is very effective. The reason it is so effective is that the technique very clearly lays out for you and the prospect in black and white the benefits of your product or service. It also serves as a great summary chart for everything you have been discussing.

You can use a T-Bar to organize the pros and cons in order to make your evaluation, as illustrated below. The pros are listed under the (+) sign and the cons under the (-) sign. I like to list out each item so the prospect can actually see line-item by line-item, each point of discussion under each heading.

Do yourself a favor. When you are presenting your product, always help the prospect with the pros, but let him develop his own cons, if there are any.

Product A

(+)	(-)
Application	Cost
Great sales team	Support
Local	Small company
Reputation	

Product B

(+)	(-)
Application	Bureaucratic
Service	Large company
Support	
Cost	
Company stability	

After looking at both alternatives, it would appear that Product B offers more pros than Product A, as well as fewer negatives than Product A. By listing out each pro and con, you now have a very good visual aid to summarize and recap the entire conversation.

Product A

(+)	(-)
+	X
+	X
+	X
	X

Product B

(+)	(-)
+	X
+	X
+	
+	
+	

The second example of Product A versus Product B does the same thing as the first example, but it only displays a checkmark for each pro and con. Use this approach if all items are equal in importance. It is less useful when trying to recap and summarize the entire conversation. Either method will work, but one method may work better than the other for you.

This technique is also good for listing out the things a prospect likes about the way he is conducting business now versus the way he would like to be able to conduct business. It can be especially effective in comparing different products, as you have just seen in the T-Bar illustrations, because it allows you to pinpoint an area of attack for your goods and services. Also, the prospect can sell to you on the pros and cons of his current method or those proposed by a competitor. Your goal is to move as many of the competitive pros as possible into the cons column by selling the added advantages of your product for that line-item on the chart. You won't get them all. What you are trying to do is to move as many of his positives as you can into his negative column.

This is also the perfect time to further qualify the prospect by asking what buying criteria he would use to make a decision. Criteria used in buying a computer would be as follows:

Price
Support
Function of software
Ease of use

Next, ask him to rank those criteria in terms of importance. How he ranks the items may be the key to your winning or losing the business. He may rearrange the list of criteria into:

Function of software
Support
Ease of use
Price

Illustration 4

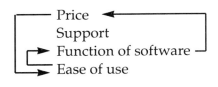

Price
Support
Function of software
Ease of use

Once you understand the buying criteria, your job becomes much easier because you now know exactly which issues you need to be selling to, and you will not waste your time on those issues that are not even a factor in the decision.

Sell only those features about your product that fulfill the prospect's requirements. Although your product may have 10,000 features, if he only needs four functions, show those four functions and forget the other 9,996. Everything else is irrelevant overkill and may just confuse him.

Although Product B appears to be the better choice on the T-Bar pros and cons, you still may have to get him to list other buying criteria, such as likes and dislikes. As an example, if liking the salesperson and doing business with a local business were more important to the buyer than cost and support, then Product A would override Product B after all.

Once he lists his likes and dislikes **along with** his buying criteria, you are in a very good position to ask him a very direct qualifying question: **"If I can show you that our product or service is equal to, or better than your current method or the other competitors' you are considering, and our product**

or service better meets your specific buying criteria, would you buy the product from me? If the answer is yes, then you know exactly what you have to do. If the answer is no, ask, "Why not?"

REFERENCE CLOSE

- When possible, reference someone who is well known and respected.

- Make certain you qualify the reference with your prospect before you do the name-dropping. You might ask his opinion of a particular reference you are about to use. Do this to make certain it isn't negative before you use that particular name as a reference.

- Also, make certain that your reference knows that he is being used as a reference and agrees to do so.

- When referencing dollar savings, it is usually better to reference percentages rather than actual numbers. That way, you do not reveal numbers that may be confidential to your customer.

Reference selling can be very effective when closing business. It sometimes gives the prospect a feeling of security just knowing that he is not the first person to try your product. There is also a certain level of comfort in knowing that he may benefit from someone else's experience. Reference selling has more impact if you reference someone whom your prospect knows and respects.

Avoiding Backfires

Of course, what may be a good reference for you may not be a good reference for your prospect. Your prospect could even be an arch rival to your reference. Always qualify your potential reference by first asking your prospect if he knows him. Get a feel for whether his attitude is positive, neutral or negative toward the reference. If it's positive or neutral, then you use the reference. If it is negative, try again with someone else more positive.

Referencing someone locally usually has more impact than referencing someone located miles away, because your prospect often may want to go see your product in use and find out how it is performing for that company – especially if it is a big-ticket item.

A reference close may go something like this:

Salesperson: "Are you familiar with Ace Manufacturing?"

Prospect: "Yes, they are one of our major competitors."

Salesperson: "How does your company compare to theirs in terms of size, growth and profit?"

Prospect: "They are much larger than we are, but two years ago we were about the same size. They are a fast-growing company. However, I don't know about their profits."

Salesperson: "Do you consider them to be a well-run company?"

Prospect: "Yes, I do."

Salesperson: "About two years ago, Ace installed one of our products. Mr. Jones attributes his significant growth to the installation of their in-house production control system, which he bought from me. You now have the opportunity to do the same thing for your company that Ace has already successfully done."

References can be very effective in helping your prospect make a decision. Who could be any better at selling your product than a satisfied user? Encourage your prospect to visit or at least call your reference to get a better appreciation for your product. Let him hear firsthand about the benefits, the usefulness, and the reliability or quality of your product or service. Someone who is a user of your product can often have much more impact on helping a prospect make a buying decision than a salesperson can ever have.

However, keep in mind that you **MUST** clear the visit in advance so that it is mutually convenient for the reference and your prospect. The last thing you want to do is surprise the company or schedule a time that will interrupt production. Make certain you know who will be interfacing with your prospect and have a good idea in advance of what he will be saying. Never drop in unannounced!

After your reference has spent his time helping you show off your product or has at least given a good testimonial, **reward him**. Send a nice letter, with another letter to the person's boss, if appropriate. Take him to dinner, invite him out for golf or tennis, or provide a night on the town for him and his spouse. Show your appreciation. You may need his help again sometime.

How to Make a Successful Demonstration

Letting your prospect see your customer using the product can also be much more effective than giving a demonstration of your own. If you do give a demonstration, it should be for the purpose of closing the sale only. Demonstrations are closing calls.

The key to giving a good demonstration is to show only what the prospect needs to see to make a commitment. You know Murphy's Law: "If it can go wrong, it will." Don't expose yourself to more potential problems than necessary.

The last thing you want is to have a demonstration not work the way you had it planned. So keep your demonstration simple and to the point. If you try to show more than required, you create an opportunity to mess something up. If he only needs to see five features, show him the five features, confirm that the five features meet the requirements as expected, and then ask for the order.

If you were buying a new air conditioner, you wouldn't want the salesperson to show you how each component of the condenser worked, would you? No!

So ask yourself, "What difference will the demo make? Do I really need to give him a demo?" If the answer is yes, then **EXACTLY and PRECISELY** what does he need to see in the demonstration to make a decision? Demo only that, and then go for the close.

ASSOCIATION CLOSE

- To test a person's value of a company or product or to get a good feel for how he views quality.

Many times when I am about to go for the close, but I know that the prospect is going to want to look around or may even be leaning toward a competitor, I use a closing technique that I call "Close by Association."

I ask him a series of questions that deal with word associations. If you take this technique and combine it with the price analogies covered earlier, you can have a dynamite set up for the close.

It may go something like this:

Salesperson: "When you think of a soft drink, what brand comes to mind?"

Prospect: "Coca-Cola."

Salesperson: "When you think of a quality champagne, what brand comes to mind?"

Prospect: "Dom Perignon."

Salesperson: "When you think of an expensive sports car, what brand comes to mind?"

Prospect: "Ferarri."

Salesperson: "When you think of a cash register, what brand come to mind?"

Prospect: "NCR."

Salesperson: "When you think of a copier, what brand comes to mind?"

Prospect: "Xerox."

Salesperson: "When you think of a computer, what brand comes to mind?"

Prospect: "IBM."

Salesperson: "If all of your responses represent quality companies to you, then why in the world would you want anything but the best for your company?"

Salesperson: "Let's do it!"

This technique can be effective only if your product is recognized as being the best or your company is recognized as the industry leader.

NEGATIVE CLOSE

- Challenge the prospect's ability to qualify or have the ability to buy.

The negative close is very dangerous. You must exercise skill and judgment in this technique. Make certain you practice on a peer before you ever attempt to try it on a prospect. I suggest that you use this type of close **ONLY** when you are losing and the only way the decision could go for you is up. Using this type of close could get you thrown out if it isn't properly executed or if you use it on the wrong type of personality.

This technique works best on the "driver" personality who likes a challenge. Many top executives have this type of personality. They are results-oriented people who like to call the shots. Many of them have large egos.

A negative close may go something like this:

Salesperson: "Mr. Smith, do you think you could afford a product of this magnitude?"

Prospect: "Afford it? Not only can I afford it, I will pay cash."

Another example might be:

Salesperson: "Mr. Jones, I am not certain that I can get you approved for credit."

Prospect: "I am certain I would qualify for credit. What information do you need?"

Often, the prospect will help you close him. He may give you several reasons why you should do business with him. People like this are usually ready to rise to the occasion when confronted with a challenge. They will take the challenge just to show you that they are in control and can do anything they darn well please, if they choose to do so.

I know of a person who is now the proud owner of a $1,500 lawn chair simply because the salesperson said, "Bob, you probably couldn't afford a chair like this." Bob fooled him! He whipped out $1,500 cash and immediately told the salesperson to write it up. Bob met the challenge.

However, your delivery of the negative close is critical. It could very well backfire on you unless you practice.

THINK IT OVER CLOSE

- Agree that there is a lot to consider.

- Gain the prospect's agreement about your product.

- Confirm his interest.

- Clarify what it isn't.

- Verify that you have satisfied his specific needs.

- Try to draw out the hidden concern when he continues to stall.

- Ask him, "Is it money?"

This type of objection may go like this:

Salesperson: "You are right, there is a lot to think about. However, do you agree that the product is easy to use?"

Prospect: "Yes."

Salesperson: "Do you agree that we can reduce your bad debt by 30 percent or $6,000 per year, and that equals $30,000 over five years?"

Prospect: "Yes."

Salesperson: "Do you agree that a 10 percent reduction in your inventory would mean about $400,000 of cash back into the business over the next five years?"

Prospect: "Yes."

Salesperson: "Do you also agree that both software packages fully meet your business requirements?"

Prospect: "Yes."

Salesperson: "Do you also agree that the return on investment meets your requirement of a 20 percent before-tax return within a 24-month period?"

Prospect: "Yes."

Salesperson:	"Based on your responses, it would appear that all the issues have been satisfied. Let's do it!"
Prospect:	"I want to think it over."
Salesperson:	"Everything appears to be right for making the investment, wouldn't you agree?"
Prospect:	"Yes, but I still want to think it over."
Salesperson:	"Let me ask you this. Is the amount of money involved an issue?"

If everything is right, what is there to think over? If the prospect still says no, then there is a very good chance **that person is not the decision maker**. Although the person may be the owner or president of the company, there is always the possibility of a silent partner who is backing the business.

If this is the case, you need to find out up front, if possible. It is terrible to say, but sometimes people will flat out lie to you about their ability to make a decision. Some people may have the responsibility of the position, without having the authority.

If the person does have the authority but still wants to continue to think it over, **his other hidden concern may be money**. Money is the second biggest obstacle to this type of stall. Cash flow or financing may be a problem, so be careful how you approach this subject. You don't want to embarrass your prospect.

You can approach this situation something like this:

Salesperson:	"Mr. Jones, everything here appears to meet or exceed your requirements. We have agreed that the system is easy to use. The software meets your requirements, and the investment is a sound financial decision based on your investment criteria and payback requirements. The only thing that we haven't really

discussed in enough depth is money. Could it be that cash flow or financing is a problem?"

Prospect: "Yes, we are currently very tight on cash."

Salesperson: "Let's take a closer look at the investment benefit and see how it may help you improve your cash flow."

This is where you move to the "you can't afford not to" close.

YOU CAN'T AFFORD NOT TO CLOSE

• Break down the cost on a per hour or per transaction basis.

• Keep it simple.

This technique will help your prospect realize how little of an investment he is really making in order to achieve such a high benefit or rate of return. If the benefit is great enough, he will help you help him acquire the product.

Example:

Let's use the scenario that we just saw in the previous technique. The benefit from a reduction in bad debt would be $30,000, and the benefit from the 10 percent inventory reduction would be $400,000, for a total benefit of $430,000. Assume the system costs $100,000. Based on an eight-hour day over five years, the system would cost the prospect $6.25 per hour to receive a benefit of $430,000.

$100,000 Investment
<u>x 34 Percent</u> (their corporate tax rate)
$ 66,000 Actual cost to consumer after taxes

Therefore, the simple breakdown cost of the system equals:

$1,100 per month over 60 months
$50.00 per day
$ 6.25 per hour

Salesperson: "That is about the cost of an employee, or maybe even a little less, especially when you consider employee benefits, etc. Would you agree?"

Prospect: "Yes."

Salesperson: "How much would you have to increase your sales to realize that type of return?"

Prospect: "Lots."

Salesperson: "Isn't it worth a $6.25 per hour investment to get a $430,000 return?"

Prospect: "Yes."

Salesperson: "Then let's do it!"

Again, you are taking away some of the mental anguish of what might be viewed as a big chunk of money or expenditure, rather than a solid $100,000 investment.

I used expenditure here instead of "investment" because it is very likely that a lot of prospects will view your product as an expense rather than a revenue generator, no matter how it is presented. If they do, it is your job to present your product at its lowest level of unit cost, and then try to redirect their thinking about your product as being a **revenue generator and an investment** instead of a cost, whenever possible.

You can also adapt this close the next time someone tells you he only has so much in the budget to spend, and you know that your product is going to be more than he has budgeted.

Learn this technique step by step and it will prove to be one of the best qualifiers you will ever use. It can turn someone who is not a prospect into an immediate buyer.

Step 1

Ask the prospect, "If you were going to invest in the stock market or if you were going to invest in a capital asset for your company, what rate of return would you look for?"

Step 2

Then ask, "Over what period of time?"

Step 3

"Is that before or after taxes?"

Step 4 **(THE CLOSE!)**

"If I understand you correctly, if I can get you X percent return after tax or before tax over the next X months, you don't care if your investment in my product costs $5 or $5 million, do you?"

If this person is a true businessman, he will tell you that you are exactly right. Ask him how much he would have to increase sales to get that type of return. How many more widgets would he have to sell to gain that much additional profit?

I know some of you are thinking that there is no way the prospect would respond like that. Let me tell you, an investment is an investment, and **if your prospect believes he can get the right kind of return, he will find the money**.

Let me give you an example that will drive the point home. The next time you run into a prospect, ask him, "Will you give me a $10 bill for a $20 bill?" See how quickly he digs into his pocket. When he brings out the $10 bill, tell him that you have another $20 bill and watch him dig for a second $10 bill. Continue this until he runs out of $10 bills. He will usually try to get you to trade for some other denomination. Tell him you will only trade for $10 bills.

Next, see how quickly he turns to someone and asks to borrow a $10 bill from him. You may also be surprised to see a bystander jump in, offering a $10 bill even before he is asked for a loan. When you ask why he jumped in, he will tell you that he saw an opportunity. The prospect will tell you the same thing. Both parties saw opportunity.

Clearly, if you can show tangible value for your product or service, the prospect will find the money, and there is usually someone else around to loan the money if he can see a profit as well.

Would you like to increase your own monthly personal expenses? Probably not. Then why in the world would you expect a company to want to increase **its** expenses? Individuals as well as companies want to reduce costs and increase income or profits. So present your product as a revenue generator whenever possible, and your success rate will climb.

By the way, since my example was a computer, you might be interested to know that studies show that companies who consider and use a computer as a revenue generator do, in fact, tend to grow more rapidly than those who view it as a necessary expense.

LOST SALE CLOSE

- When everything else has failed.

- It must be something you have done or have not been able to communicate.

Some people call this technique the "Columbo" close. What you call it isn't important. What is important is to understand that this approach can completely turn the situation around once you have been told that you are not going to be the vendor of choice.

When you find out that your competitor is going to get the order instead of you, but the prospect has not yet given him a firm order, you very simply and very professionally thank him for his time and cooperation. Tell him it has been a pleasure working with him and that you wish him the very best with the product he chose.

However, there is just one thing that you want to ask before you go. Ask him, "If an opportunity presents itself to compete for your business in the future, or if there is an opportunity to compete for another segment of your business, would you allow me to come back and compete for the business?" Seek his commitment to allow you to do so. When he gives you that commitment (or even if he doesn't), thank him for his time and leave.

In the television show "Columbo," Columbo could never seem to leave the room because there was always something puzzling him. Like Columbo, you can turn around and walk back to the prospect and say something like this:

Salesperson: "Fred, before I leave, could I ask you to do me a personal favor?"

Prospect: "Sure. What is it?"

Salesperson: "I need your help. There are a lot of people that I could go to, but of all the people here, I respect your opinion the most. There is one thing that I have learned about you since we first met. You tell it like it is and won't hold back on anything. Because of that, I know you will give me a straight and honest answer. Am I correct?"

Prospect: "That's right. I certainly will."

Salesperson: "Next week, I have an opportunity to present a similar proposal to another prospect that I have been working with. I want to make certain that I don't lose that opportunity. Will you tell me what I really did wrong here so I won't do it again?"

Prospect: "Well, John, I don't think you did anything wrong. In fact, I would like to be able to do business with you.

However, when you gave us the demonstration, we saw how you tracked raw materials through work in process and rolled up the cost into the finished product. Our operation is a little more complex than that. We sometimes take raw material, and part way through the process, that piece goes back into inventory with a new part number. It may become a component part that goes into a different product or sub-assembly and never makes it all the way to finished goods on the first pass through production."

Salesperson: "Fred, are you telling me that if I had been able to properly demonstrate to you that we could do that, you would have bought the system from me?"

Prospect: "Sure."

Salesperson: "Is that the only reason that you decided not to do business with me?"

Prospect: "Yes, I assumed you couldn't provide that capability."

Salesperson: "Fred, I apologize. I am very sorry that we missed that concern. In fact, we do that function very effectively. Fred, this is probably going to be one of the bigger decisions that your company will make this year, is that right?"

Prospect: "Yes."

Salesperson: "Then what you are telling me, Fred, is that you are going to make the recommendation to buy the other system based on the lack of information or poor demonstration that I gave you?"

Prospect: "Well, I guess that I am."

Salesperson: "Fred, I certainly don't want to put you in that position, and I don't want to be put in that position. If that is the only reason you are about to choose the other product, would you at least give me another couple of hours to show you exactly how our system handles that function, especially since this is going to be one of the biggest decisions your company will make this year?"

Prospect: "I don't think so. You had your chance just like every-one else. I have spent all the time looking that I am going to spend."

Salesperson: "I fully understand how you feel, and I can appreciate that. However, since this decision is so critical and you will be living with this decision for the next sev-eral years, isn't it worth spending another couple of hours to validate a decision of this magnitude?"

Prospect: "Okay. Two hours and that's it!"

Salesperson: "Thank you, Fred. You don't know how much I appreciate your giving me a second chance to make up for what I failed to do the first time. I guess we were just so involved with so many things going on at once, that I completely missed what may have been the most significant issue to you. To ensure that doesn't happen again, **EXACTLY and PRE-CISELY** what is it that you need to see to convince you that we can, in fact, perform this requirement to your satisfaction?"

What you have just done is stroked the prospect and humbled yourself for being inadequate. This approach, asking for someone's help, may just put the real objection on the table or draw out an objection that had not previously surfaced. If that happens, then you have just opened yourself up for an opportunity to once again start selling.

The key point is that this may be the very first time the real objec-tion comes out in the open. This technique may not work in every case, but if it works occasionally, you are doing better than had you not tried it.

You may never get this far with the prospect. However, a couple of minutes ago you didn't have an order or a commission check coming. You had lost the business opportunity. It is times like this when you need to get creative and start thinking outside the square.

Have you ever liked someone but felt that he was incompetent? You may have. Maybe in the eyes of your prospect, **you** are that incompetent person, but because he liked you, he wouldn't say anything to hurt your feelings. There could have been any number of reasons for his decision not to buy. Maybe you were just out-sold.

This technique gives you an opportunity to get a second shot. Now that you have laid your cards on the table, you can only trust that the prospect will be open and honest with you.

Look for some type of objection to surface that may enable you to continue the selling process and not be shut out. Regardless of what surfaces, it could trigger something that could reopen the door for you and make the selling opportunity a whole new ball game.

After reviewing these 12 closing techniques, pick out five or six that you feel you could easily adapt to your personality and style. Then, **PRACTICE, PRACTICE, PRACTICE** these techniques until they become as natural as breathing to you.

Remember, you are the most important part of the selling process, and **YOUR** choice of techniques can make the difference in whether a prospect will do business with your company or someone else.

CHAPTER 11

HOW TO HANDLE MAJOR DELAYS

Despite all of the rules and techniques for qualifying, overcoming objections and closing that you have learned so far, I hope you are beginning to understand that gaining a commitment is seldom a standard formula. I challenge you now to **test your knowledge and creativity** against the major purchasing delays below. These delays are only stalls or another objection to overcome. Stop at each heading and see if you can correctly anticipate the tips you might apply in that situation. Then scan the material for many familiar points you can use as review.

Once you have gone through the entire selling process and you can't get a commitment from the prospect, what do you think the problem might be? If everything is right and there is absolutely no reason for him not to purchase your product, you will usually find that he doesn't have the authority to make a decision.

THE BUYER LACKS AUTHORITY TO MAKE DECISION

Many salespeople find themselves spending a lot of time providing information to a prospect. Sometimes days and weeks go by before the salesperson realizes that the person does not have the authority to make a decision.

It is essential to know right up front who will be making the final decision. Don't be afraid to ask! Then make a call on that person.

One more tip for your initial sales call: Once you get authorization to work within an account, make certain you cater to everyone you can! Sometimes the person who seems to be the **least likely** to ever be in a buying position, ends up being promoted. You never know when one of those people will be in a position of authority or have the opportunity to help you out in the future. Your future support could depend on the relationships you have developed along the way. So make friends throughout the account. You certainly don't want to offend or slight anyone. Although he may not have the power to buy today, he may be instrumental in supporting your recommendation. Tomorrow, he may have the authority to make buying decisions. Therefore, don't burn any bridges along the way.

Ask very directly, "Who will be making the final decision?"

AVAILABLE FINANCING

If the prospect does have the authority to make a decision but still won't commit, the problem could be money. Money is the second biggest reason for delay. Even if money is the root of all evil, you still can't acquire much without it. It is easy for someone to say, "It is too expensive," or "I can't afford it," and exit without buying.

Some individuals or companies inevitably will be cash constrained or over-extended. No matter how badly they would like to have your product, the funds may not be available. If you are able to show how your product can help **reduce** his current cost or improve his cash flow, then maybe the **two of you** can come up with a creative way to leverage his ability to acquire your product.

If the potential sale is big enough, explore several avenues for financing at his firm and yours. If the prospect has used up his line of credit at the bank, perhaps your company could offer some type of financing program or you could arrange third-party financing for him. Maybe your company would be willing to floor plan (help finance) your product for him or put your product on consignment.

I strongly urge you to become knowledgeable of tax laws, especially if the purchase of your product has an impact on tax liabilities.

That knowledge alone can set you apart from your competitor. After all, as a salesperson, it is your job to help your prospect acquire your product. You can be far ahead of your nearest competitor if you can double as a financial consultant and show him how your product could help offset his tax liability. It also enhances your image as a professional, and that, too, will convert into added sales.

Ask him, "Would you buy or invest in my product if money or financing were not a problem?" If he answers yes, then see what you can do about solving the problem.

BUYER NEEDS MORE INFORMATION

If you are talking to the decision maker and he has the money, and you still can't get a commitment, maybe all of his questions haven't been answered. A hidden obstacle hasn't surfaced. One of the major delays in a buying decision is due to lack of the right information. You may provide your prospect with a ton of data that may have absolutely nothing to do with the information he needs to help him decide. That is why it is important to question his buying criteria.

You want to have a **well-informed buyer**. You need to be certain your prospect understands the benefits of your product well enough so that when he buys, there are no surprises. It is nice to get a quick sell, but if the buyer later finds that the product doesn't do what he bought it for, he is going to at least be disappointed, if not irate. The last thing you want to do is to create an unhappy and angry customer. When you have a dissatisfied customer, you can almost always count on him to badmouth you, your product and your company.

Sometimes, even though he may have enough information to make a decision, he may still want to shop around for alternatives. When this happens, what do you do?

You can often eliminate this delay if you are knowledgeable enough about your competitors and can accurately contrast the two products by pointing out the strengths of yours. **NEVER** run down or disparage your competitor! It will only make you look bad in the eyes of the prospect. **Sell the benefits of your product.** Use the pro and con T-Bar approach to help the prospect come to his own logical conclusion. Let the prospect conclude for himself that the competition's product is inferior or doesn't offer the same advantages as your product. Help lead him to that conclusion through the proper questioning we discussed earlier, then go for the commitment.

Specifically ask him, "What information do you need to make a decision?"

THE PROSPECT JUST ISN'T SOLD

Many times you get a prospect who is wishy-washy. He needs reassurance. Maybe he would buy your product if he fully understood what it is, what it did, how it works or how he could use it to his benefit. He just isn't sold. When this happens, the best thing to do is to ask point blank, "What is it that's bothering you about my product?" You might say:

"It appears that something is troubling you. Is it something that I didn't clearly explain, or maybe something that you don't fully understand? Have I failed to address some issue or concern?" Wait for the reply, and he doesn't open up to you and explain what he is thinking, start probing by asking him open-ended questions. This should draw out the real objection so you can proceed.

Ask if he would like to talk to or see someone using your product or service. Urge him to just try your product or service on a trial basis.

THE DELAY IS DESTINED

What do you do if the company is being sold or being acquired by another firm? Maybe the company is going into receivership. Maybe their line of credit isn't good. Maybe they don't have the money, or funding isn't available. If you encounter any of these issues, don't immediately walk away. See if you or your company can do anything to help, especially if the prospect really wants your product and you want his business.

Be patient and remain in touch in case the scenario changes. As a result, you will often find a new, loyal prospect waiting for you when the time is right.

If he shows interest in your product, ask, "How would you suggest that **WE** work around this situation?"

PRIOR CONTRACTUAL COMMITMENT

Another delay you may face is due to prior contractual agreements. Unless these agreements are about to expire, you probably won't get very far unless you have a way to help your prospect out of the contract. Sometimes he is willing to pay the penalties to buy his way out of a contract just to free himself from the vendor. Some suppliers may choose to buy out another contract based on the business opportunity they will receive from the prospect. However, if you can't get their business today, you can certainly be paving the way to be their vendor of choice once their contract is terminated. So, again, don't give in or give up. Stay in touch.

If possible, give your prospect a sample of your product or service so he can compare your offering to his existing product or service. Ask what you would have to do to be awarded the next contract.

BUYER'S REMORSE

All of us at one time or another have experienced the feeling of deciding we should have bought something else. After we got home, maybe we realized we didn't really need it in the first place. Maybe we realized we couldn't really afford it when we received the statement. Maybe we just realized we really could have done without it. It was nice, but not essential – and we don't want to put ourselves in that situation again.

When you sense this dilemma with your prospect, ask him to try the product or service. It also helps to put him in touch with others who had similar feelings before they bought. Sometimes, first selling the spouse or partner, and then using him or her as your inside salesperson works, too.

GUILT AND ANXIETY

Guilt and anxiety are other reasons for not buying. Guilt is the anger we direct at ourselves for something we have done and for which we are responsible. You know how people say they feel guilty for eating a candy bar when they are on a diet. The next time they start to pick up a candy bar, they will turn and walk away. It may not be any different for the prospect when it comes to buying your product than it is for the person buying the candy. Rather than feel guilty about the acquisition, they may walk away.

There is also the chance that the prospect may feel guilty in acquiring your product because there are other items that might be needed more. Your item may not be a priority. Or, the prospect could feel anxious about the payment he may be facing.

Reassurance is the key factor when this feeling surfaces. Reiterate all of the positives and the benefits as strongly and as simply as you can. And again, offer a product trial when appropriate.

THE PROSPECT DOESN'T LIKE YOUR COMPANY

What if the prospect doesn't like your company? Think back to the earlier discussion: If people buy from people they like, then you have to sell yourself. For most people, **the salesperson is the company**. Ask your prospect why he feels the way he does, and let him completely vent his frustrations or opinions before you try to respond. This will defuse and neutralize the situation, and he will usually become less hostile or negative toward you.

Your question shows that you are empathetic and concerned about his attitude and how he feels. Let him know that you are there to help change the situation. Tell him that it will be like reconciling a marriage: First you have bitterness and maybe hatred, then heavenly bliss! Hopefully, you can help bring back a little bliss if you take on the role of "statesman."

Many people believe a company is only as good as its worst employee. Maybe the salesperson who called on this prospect before was one of the less capable employees. Now the prospect holds bad feelings toward the company. Try not to let yourself be penalized as a result of another individual's action. Make certain you are the best that you can be. It will pay great dividends to you in the long run.

By being positive and competent and effectively selling yourself, you may completely change the prospect's attitude about your company.

THE PROSPECT DOESN'T LIKE YOU

Heaven forbid! I know this couldn't be you! But, possibly, just possibly, could **you** be the problem? I hope not, but occasionally you will find that someone does not like you and refuses to do business with you.

What do you do when someone wants your product, but refuses to buy it because they don't like you as a salesperson? A lot of times there isn't anything that you can do if the prospect just walks off. On the other hand, you can sometimes turn the situation around if you can get the prospect to realize this is a business situation and not allow the personalities to get involved. If they respect the person professionally, many times people will buy from people they don't like. This is especially true if it is to the prospect's benefit to acquire your product or service. As soon as possible, get the discussion on a positive business level.

If you still see that your prospect isn't going to do business with you on a professional basis, then you may want to turn the sale over to someone else. You may want to do it right away if you see a conflict beginning to surface. Everyone can win as a result. The chemistry between the prospect and the other person may be better, and your company will still get the business. If you are in a commissioned sales job, you may still get part or all of the commission. The extra effort on your part could mean the difference in the sale.

Try to remember that each time you encounter a prospect you don't immediately like, he may turn out to be one of your best customers.

Have you ever met someone whom **you didn't like** when you first met them? You probably have. Then over a period of time, he became one of your best friends. How long did it take for that relationship to evolve into something positive?

This may be a new and strange twist to your marketing approach, but **there are also a few prospects out there that you may not want to have as a customer**. They can never be satisfied and are always causing you and your company problems. These are the prospects that you want your competitors to have. While your competitor is trying to fix their problems day in and day out, you can be selling to the better prospects and, as a result, keeping your competitors off the street and out of your territory.

––––––––––

The reasons just stated above for **not** buying are not the only reasons for delays, but they do represent the more common delays you should anticipate. When confronted with these situations, it is up to you to be prepared and determine which approach of handling the obstacle is the most effective for you.

CHAPTER 12

TIPS FOR THE CLOSE

Before the Call

- Be prepared. Have your closing prepared and rehearsed **before** you make the call.

- Know the background and personality of the decision maker or decision makers.

- Have a peer review and critique your presentation before you present your proposal.

- Have the order or letter of intent written in advance.

- Have contracts filled out in advance.

- Have references available.

During the Call

- Have sources of financing available when applicable.

- If possible, try to close the business when you have the prospect on your turf or some neutral turf, rather than his own.

- Open with the close – "When I have finished with my presentation and addressed all of your issues and concerns, I am going to ask you to invest in my product."

- If you are giving a closing demo, show only those functions he needs to see to confirm that your product satisfies his requirements or needs.

- Watch his body language for buying signals.

- Listen to his words, comments and questions for closing opportunities.

- Try to understand what motivates the decision maker.

- Be prepared to answer any question and handle any objections.

- Be crisp, neat and to the point.

- Be able to show the benefit to the prospect (both tangible and intangible).

- Be able to show the added value of doing business with you and your company.

- Let someone else sell for you when appropriate. Use someone well known who supports your product or service, and is respected.

- Ask the prospect to buy. Use the most direct approach.

- If the final answer is negative, ask: "What did I do wrong that I was unable to gain your business?"

After the Close

- Tell him what you are going to do, then do it.

- If follow-up is required, tell him what to expect and when to expect it.

- If he needs to do anything in the interim, tell him what it is.

- When he does make the commitment to buy, ask for a referral or the name of someone else he may know who would like to own a product like the one he just purchased. This is the time most buyers want others "in the boat" with them or would like for one of their friends or colleagues to be able to participate in the same type of acquisition.

- Thank him for his business and promptly leave. (You don't need to hang around after you get an order. You might say something that would prompt him to change his decision.)

- If a decision is delayed, phone back. Never ask: "What have you decided?" because if the answer was yes, he would have called you already. You need to continue selling. "There was something I failed to mention about the _____." **Always make it a new selling opportunity!** Start where you left off before, and continue to go for the close.

CHAPTER 13

CLOSING PHRASES THAT GET RESULTS

Below are dozens of oral cues you can use to move the sale forward. Review these until they become automatic to you in making the sale.

125 Helpful Closing Phrases:

- I am confident ...

- I am convinced ...

- I believe ...

- Let's do it!

- Let's go ahead!

- Let's get started!

- I recommend we do it!

- I would like to have your decision ...

- Tell me where we stand.

- I need your approval to go ahead with this order.

- I would like your approval to proceed.

- I would like your decision today.

- I am going to ask for your commitment/support.

- You are going to love it!

- In order to confirm a delivery date, we need you to okay this tentative order.

- There is no real reason why we should not proceed immediately with the order and implementation.

- How soon could you take delivery?

- Will you be paying cash, or will you be financing the purchase?

- When would you like to start realizing the benefits?

- When do you want to be operational?

- Which color do you prefer?

- Would you like a trial period?

- Would you like to try the product?

- That's quite a return, isn't it?

- Isn't this a worthwhile investment?

- Will you okay this order?

- All right, Mr. _____, right here if you please?

- Would you prefer ...?

- Can you see how it saves you money?

- Are you interested in saving money?

- If you are ever going to start saving money, when would you like to start receiving the benefits?

- What date would you prefer delivery?

- Which size would you prefer?

- The next step from here is to place the product on order and start the implementation plan.

- By signing this letter, you are authorizing us to begin the implementation plan with your company.

- Can we confirm your order now and start planning your installation?

- Please sign here.

- You have agreed to all the benefits and justification. Let's get started.

- You have agreed that our product will provide you with the benefits you are looking for. Let's order it.

- I have shown you a product that meets your requirements and is cost-justified, so let's put the product on order so we can start implementation.

- Cash or charge?

- There is no doubt in your mind that this product will do everything that you wanted it to do. Let's do it.

- Is there any reason why you wouldn't put this on order today?

- This product has everything you want except one thing – a home, let's do it.

- Since we're both in agreement that this is the right solution for you and it's cost-justified, let's go ahead and place it on order.

- I would like to place a position order, which is absolutely no commitment from you, but enables me to get in the queue for an early ship date.

- Mr. _____ , now that we have found the right solution for you, if I can get you to please sign this contract, I will place the equipment on order today.

- Which document should I bring with me ... the purchase order or term lease document?

- How soon would you like to be operational?

- Who will be attending the installation planning class with you?

- Let's put the equipment on order so we can begin the implementation and training of your staff.

- As per the goals you originally set out to accomplish, we have determined a way to improve your bottom line. When can we deliver your equipment?

- When you have this equipment installed, I am sure that you will receive the benefits that we discussed.

- Therefore, will you please sign this agreement so we can begin your coverage?

- We've done our job, and we've done the homework. In order to start realizing the $_____ benefit, let's do business and get the system on order today.

- Let's not lose any more of the benefits we've identified. Let's start realizing those benefits today. Let's do business.

- What else remains to be done for me to earn your business?

- Go with the best company in the _____ industry, so you can become the best company in your industry.

- Your proposal expires at the end of the week. Let's move ahead.

- We have presented a solution that we both agree will provide the benefits you are looking for – is there any reason why we can't put the policy in place starting today?

- We've agreed on the benefits that you'll receive. Let's put in an order.

- We need to get the ball rolling on this. We need to get a position order. Can you sign an order today?

- We've determined that this is the solution you need – and we need to get it ordered today.

- As you have agreed, the proposed product is a great solution. Would you please authorize the shipment?

- Now that I have provided you with the solution you asked for and showed you the cost benefits, may we place the order today?

- If I can get you to sign this please?

- May I have your okay to order the product?

- Let's get it on order today – sign here.

- You and I both know you need this product. Let's order it today.

- Would you like to pay cash up front or go with our financing plan?

- If we have covered all the bases, will you authorize an order?

- Can I get you to sign an order?

- Would you like to use your pen or mine to sign right here?

- After you sign right here, which offering would you like as your bonus?

- Now that you have agreed with the benefits that the product can provide, will you please sign the order letter so you can start realizing those savings ASAP?

- I have met the requirements you had set forth. The sooner you place the system on order, the sooner you can start realizing the benefits we've just discussed.

- (Have a positional letter of intent prepared to slide across the table). All we need to move ahead is your signature.

- Is there anything standing between my having an order placed or authorized today?

- If there is nothing else to be resolved, can we have the order?

- Can we place the _____ on order?

- Can we begin scheduling deliveries?

- I have a _____ reserved for you. When do you want it?

- To ensure timely delivery, let's go ahead and put your _____ order in now.

- It seems we have met all your requirements. Can I place your order today?

- Now that we've shown you how you can cut your inventory and increase your cash flow, don't you think we should get the system on order?

- You agree that this solution handles all your objectives. Now let's get it on order.

- I'd like to take this opportunity to thank you for your business and let you know the next step. We'd like to begin training on _____.

- You've agreed that if we did_____, that you would put a system on order. We've now done these things. I believe it's time for us to move forward.

- Mr. _____, which options (or features) should I include on your _____?

- Is there any reason we shouldn't put the _____ on order?

- When do we need to be up and operational on this?

- We can have you completely converted in one month. When would you like to get started?

- If I can show you how we can save you money and increase profits, will you place an order with me today?

- As you can see, for the cost of a minimum wage employee, we can meet your requirements, so let's get the machine hired! Sign here.

- Do you agree that I've met the requirements? Have I addressed your concerns? Would you like to use my pen?

- Now that you have agreed to the benefits and justification of this _____, may I place one on order for you?

- Are there any needs or concerns which we have not addressed? If not ....

- Is there anything else I can show you or answer any other questions before you sign with us?

- What would it take to get you to sign with us today?

- Is there anything we haven't already gone over that would prevent you from signing with us today?

- We've addressed all the criteria you set forth in your product requirements, by either taking the product as is or with minor modifications. Will you sign this order so we can meet your deadline?

- What else do I have to do to earn your business?

- Let's get this on order now before the price increases.

- Since we have addressed all your concerns, let's go ahead and sign the order.

- Since you have no more questions or concerns, can we get the _____ in ASAP?

- Since you agree the product will increase your revenue 20 percent, let's set the installation date.

- Since we agree this system will meet your needs of reducing expenses 10 percent, while raising profits 15 percent, let's set a date to make this product operational in your account.

- The previous justification shows a payback of less than two years, which beats your purchase criteria significantly. Can we place the _____ on order for you today?

- You have just seen that for every day you are not using this _____, it is costing you significant money. Don't you feel we should get the order in ASAP?

- Do you agree that my solution addresses your concerns? Then can we put the _____ on order for you?

- In order for you to gain the benefits of your new _____, let's put it on order now.

- Have you seen anything here today that would prevent you from placing an order today?

- Is there any other information you need in order to make a decision?

- Since I have answered all of your concerns, is there any reason why you won't sign this document?

- Let's get this _____ on order today and start making more money now.

- Here's the best part of buying a _____, – actually ordering it and making you happy.

- The next step is really easy. Sign here and I'll place the order.

- You have agreed to the benefits and the money you'll save. Let's get it on order before it costs you any more.

- We look forward to further developing our partnership with you. When would you like to begin our relationship?

- Just do it!

- If you will type the order letter right now, I'll deliver it to _____ today and get the ball rolling.

- If I understand you correctly, our next step is to sign the contracts.

- I need you and you need me. Let's do it as a team.

- We need to place the order today if we are going to avoid the price increase that is about to occur.

- The sale ends tomorrow. Shall I go ahead and add this to your account?

CHAPTER 14

HOW TO AVOID SELF-SABOTAGE

Your Attitude

We have already talked about buyer attitudes and all of the techniques you can use to guide those attitudes toward a close. Now we need to talk about **YOUR** attitude. Your attitude also can be critical in making a sale. In fact, your attitude is even more critical than your prospect's.

The degree of success you can attain depends a lot on your attitude and drive. You must be self-motivated if you are going to be really successful. Many times you have to create your own opportunity. You need the self-confidence to get others to envision your ideas as reality. You have to get people to believe in you. More important, you have to believe in yourself. Success in sales is no different than success in sports. First you have to visualize being successful in your mind. Then you have to visualize making the call. Once you have gone over it in your mind enough times, you then need to execute the call. It is only a matter of doing it! After a while, it will become second nature to you.

What makes one salesperson successful and another one unsuccessful? A successful salesperson is creative and will try new techniques that another salesperson would never do. He lives day to day on the edge. He continues to push his limits and abilities.

A successful salesperson always sees opportunity, even in a down economy. When times get tough, good salespeople dig in. There is a saying that, **"Tough times never last, but tough people do."** Another saying is, **"When the going gets tough, the tough**

get going." That is the attitude you need to have in order to be a really good salesperson. You can't allow people to just blow you off. You need to dig in and ask more questions. Then decide whether or not you have a qualified prospect. **You** need to do the qualifying – not them.

If you have desire, tenacity, determination and a positive attitude, you may find there isn't a mountain high enough or prospect mean enough that you can't conquer. And the financial rewards can be staggering.

Your attitude needs to be positive and upbeat. You should display an attitude of empathy, poise and professionalism. Above all, you need to project an **ATTITUDE OF ACTION**! You want to be viewed as a person who makes things happen, as opposed to one who lets things happen. You can make it happen! Remember: **Until some-one says "NO" or gives you an objection, your job really hasn't begun.** As Winston Churchill once said, "Sometimes your best isn't good enough. Sometimes you have to do what is required."

As a salesperson, you never want to flaunt your dirty laundry, complaints or frustrations in front of prospects. A negative attitude can only hurt you, because, however you feel about your company, to that prospect you are the company!

On the other hand, a positive attitude can open doors to opportu-nities that you never before thought possible. As an example, the owner of a shoe manufacturing plant sent his twin sons to two dif-ferent islands to look for new business opportunities so they might keep their plant operating. The first son called back and said, "Dad, we better plan on shutting the plant down because the people on this island don't even wear shoes." The second son called back and said, "Dad, get ready to expand production. These people don't wear shoes, and we are going to be first in the marketplace!"

Same situation, different attitude. **An opportunity is all in how you view it.** It has been said that, "It is your attitude, not your aptitude, that determines your altitude."

We all have bad days when we just don't feel very motivated. When you have days like that, you just want to stay in bed and away from prospects and customers. When I have one of those days, I will pick up the phone and call on some of my worst prospects. These are people that I know will never buy anything from me. I will call up five or 10 of them just to get myself fired up and motivated.

Masochism, you say? Not at all. It is doing whatever it takes to get motivated. After getting **fired up** from continuous rejection, I then call on a qualified prospect. Being of the "driver" type personality, I'm personally motivated by the challenge of a rejection. You should determine what motivates you. You will be surprised how effective you can be once you get motivated and get **YOUR** attitude right.

I work by a very simple philosophy that keeps me going every day: "I have more 'butt' than you have teeth, so start chewing." There is nothing that a prospect can say or do that is going to offend me.

If you as a salesperson take rejection in the business world personally, you will lose your effectiveness. You have to realize up front that you are not going to sell your product or service to everyone you meet. In fact, you are probably going to get a lot of negative responses every time you ask for a buying decision. As a result, I can't stress enough how essential a positive, enthusiastic and self-confident attitude is in helping you be successful.

People are persuaded much more by the depth of your conviction than the height of your logic. Your enthusiasm is the best proof you can exhibit. **If you can't get excited about your product, how in the world is your prospect going to get excited about it?** As a salesperson, your job is to persuade other people to take a course of action.

It's a simple fact that enthusiasm can help make the sale. Have you ever bought anything that you could not justify? Maybe it was an expensive toy such as a boat, a recreational vehicle, a camper, a designer dress, jewelry, fur or some such item. Once you bought the article, psychologically what happened? You began finding ways to justify how you could afford it and why it was a smart thing to purchase!

People naturally like to acquire and own things. A successful salesperson will help them get excited and find ways to own the product. In fact, if they don't buy, they will still go through the same process of rationalization and tell themselves why it was good that they didn't buy the product or service.

The Biggest Obstacle of All

If you are the most important part of the sales process, what do you think is your biggest obstacle in the sales process?

YOU!

You are your own worst enemy! You are the one who can make the difference in whether someone buys your product or not. You are the one who can either **make** or **break** a sale.

Remember, in sales, **YOU, YOUR ACTIONS, WHAT YOU SAY, HOW YOU SAY IT, THE EFFORT YOU PUT FORTH and YOUR ATTITUDE** can be the difference in whether a prospect decides to make a purchase from you or not.

Too many salespeople fall into the habit of self-sabotage without realizing it. Some of the more common mistakes are listed below. Review them. Think about them. Then **avoid** them to ensure that you're not your own worst enemy on your next sales call.

The Five Most Common Mistakes

1. **We get away from the basics.** If your success declines, get back to the basics. Mistakes often occur when veteran salespeople become complacent after a period of time. Even though they may have been well trained, they tend to get away from what they have already learned. This is no different than a pro golfer who starts hitting bad shots. One of the first things a pro golfer will do is go back to the basics and progress from that point until he gets his swing

back "into the groove." As a professional salesperson, you often need to do the same thing.

I learned this lesson the first time I went to my company's Sales School to be a guest calltaker. I quickly realized by the end of the first day that I didn't sell like this any more. I had become complacent and one of the good old boys. As a result, I had gotten away from the basics of asking for the business.

I immediately changed my attitude and technique of selling when I returned to the territory. The results were overwhelming. I knew how to do it. I had just gotten away from **doing** what I knew how to do.

2. **We don't listen.** I believe enough has been said on this issue. However, if you think back over the years, you will probably say that one of the biggest reasons you always got in trouble was for not listening. When you don't listen, it can project a bad image to your prospect. And, that can cost you money.

3. **We don't read the signals.** Another area where we need to be vigilant is having the ability to read body language and other physical expressions that can tip us off as to what a prospect may be thinking. If a person nods his head, that signals concurrence or disagreement. If a person moves forward in his chair, you generally have his interest. If he moves back in his chair and folds his arms, he is usually less interested and tends to be on the defensive. If he frowns, he is in disagreement or may not clearly understand what you are saying.

You need to know when "no" means "no" and when "no" means "maybe" or "yes." Do you remember when your parents used to tell you no? "No" meant that you had better not do it or you would be in big trouble. You also knew when "no" meant that you could get away with it this time and not get in trouble. Stay aware of body language and be able to read your prospect to determine if what he says is what he means.

4. **We overkill with irrelevant information.** Too much data can kill a sale, especially irrelevant data. Some salespeople feel that they have to know everything there is to know about their company, including the complete history of the organization, the players, how long the company has been in business, support structures, product lines, how the product works, etc. Even though they may know all of this information, it may have little value in helping them close the sale. Why? You can be a technical giant or rocket scientist in each of these areas, but if you can't present your product or service at a level the prospect understands and relates to, then you are not effectively communicating with your prospect and end up wasting everyone's time.

If your company or product has a feature, then there should be some tangible **benefit** of this feature as it relates to your prospect's need. Otherwise, don't dwell on it.

Do you own a watch? If you do, do you know how it works? Do you even care? What do you care about? Exactly, you want to know if it keeps accurate time. The same thing applies to selling. If you sell watches, few people care that you may know all the integral parts of a watch and how the movements work. They only came in to buy one, not build one.

Think about how you present your product or service to the prospect. It is nice that you may know how it works, but most people really don't care. Give them the information they need to make a buying decision and move on to someone else.

5. **We don't ask for the order.** Believe it or not, the single greatest mistake salespeople make is, that they do not ask for the order. The main reason for this is that no one likes to be told **"NO"** and have the feeling of rejection.

Sometimes a salesperson is hesitant to ask someone to buy because he feels the cost of his product is a large amount of money. However, if the salesperson has done his job and properly cost-justified his product and its benefits, why should he care how much it costs?

What appears to be a large sum of money to some of us may be petty cash to others. Some companies and some people don't have to ask anyone for approval to make an acquisition. Some companies allow members of their organization to make acquisitions without even getting a signature sign-off from top management or obtaining committee approval. If you have justified your product or service to meet their investment criteria, then you have earned the right to ask for the business.

You have to realize that you are going to get a lot of no's before you get a yes. The more people you approach and ask to buy, the better your chances of getting someone to say, "I'll take it!"

Make it a point to learn from your mistakes and adjust your approach as a result of each lesson. Rehearse and experiment with new approaches and see how they work for you.

Work Smart

I challenge you to evaluate how you spend your time each day. There is absolutely no direct correlation between working long hours and success, or between working hard and success. Neither is there a correlation between working short hours and being a failure. The bottom line when it comes to closing business and making money is to work smart. I am certain that there are salespeople who are already at work when you arrive each morning and are still there after you go home each day. By the same token, there are probably salespeople who come to work long after you have arrived and leave long before you ever get ready to go home.

Are both of these types successful? They certainly can be. The only difference is that one may work a lot **smarter** than the other.

To work smart, evaluate how much time you are spending in each area of your business: direct customer contact, administration, travel, planning, proposals, telephone conversations, personal business, etc. As you think about what you do each day, ask yourself how effective you are in performing each activity, and see how much time you are spending on each of those activities.

Figure out how much your time is worth. When you do, you will start viewing your job differently. You will even approach your daily activities differently, once you realize how much nonproductive time you may be wasting in the different areas. Remember, your time is money, so invest it wisely.

I can assure you of one thing. If you are paid on 100 percent commission, you will view an opportunity differently than someone who is on salary or salary-plus. If you are on salary or salary-plus, you might want to reassess how you would be spending your time with some of your current prospects if you were on 100 percent commission. You would be asking the tough questions up front and be doing a much better job qualifying their propensity to buy. You would not allow yourself to be jerked around by the prospect or customer. You would not latch on to someone and waste a lot of your time with him if you knew he was not a buyer. That is how the race horse salesperson needs to think as he is out there trying to conquer market share.

Don't get discouraged if you don't sell something the first day or even the first few months. If you are determined, persistent and trainable, success will eventually be there. It takes time to adjust to a new sales job or new territory. It may take you awhile to get acclimated to all of the things you need to learn and know. But once you gain the skills and confidence you need, success will start to happen. The way you gain that confidence is to just go out there, get beat up and get your head kicked in a few more times. After you do that, you will eventually figure out what works best for you. Again, it will take you some time to gain the experience and confidence you need, so don't get discouraged.

Self-Check Yourself

I'd like to share a couple of other quick tips that will help you to be more productive.

About halfway through the call, ask yourself this question: "As a result of where this conversation is going **right now**, am I going to walk out of here with an order?"

If the answer is no, ask yourself a second question: "As a result of what I am doing right now, am I setting myself up to get an order in the **future**?" If the answer is yes, then ask: "What questions do I need to be asking in order to move the future to **NOW**?"

It also helps to do a call review after you talk to each prospect and assess what you did right and what you did wrong. Determine what you could have done differently to have made the call go better. Then do it differently the next time and see if it works.

Over time, you will discover what works best for you. And you will soon be on your way to realizing the type of income that few other professions have to offer.

It is Now Up to You

YOUR SUCCESS IS ENTIRELY UP TO YOU. You are the one who makes things happen. It is up to you to gain the commitment from your prospect. Above all, to be productive, **ALWAYS ASK FOR THE ORDER!**

One closing point: **WHATEVER YOU DO, DO IT RIGHT THE FIRST TIME!** It saves you so much time and effort when you take the time to do it right the first time. Not only that – your prospect will have a much better image of both you and your company. Wouldn't you prefer to do business with someone who comes across as professional, someone who knows his business and his product, someone who takes the time to understand your needs and wants before he starts selling you something? I challenge you to think about that the next time you talk with a prospect.

We are all searching for the formula for success. We all measure success differently. For the salesperson:

SUCCESS IS GOING FROM FAILURE TO FAILURE WITHOUT LOSS OF ENTHUSIASM

If you happen to be a student of the Bible, you know that God gave Joshua the formula for success almost 2,000 years ago. God told

Joshua many times over: **IF YOU WANT TO BE SUCCESSFUL, YOU MUST BE STRONG AND COURAGEOUS! DO NOT TREMBLE OR BE DISMAYED. BANISH FEAR AND DOUBT.** He also told Joshua to learn how to be a servant. This can be the formula for success for a salesperson. You have to be strong and courageous, as well as banish all fear and doubt about not being successful. If you provide good service to your customers, they will reward you accordingly with orders. They will take care of you if you take care of them. If you approach your career with this attitude, you will be a success, and as a result, you will earn more money.

If you find this profession isn't for you, don't worry about it. Why? Because you can marry more money in five minutes than you can earn in a lifetime.

I hope this has been fun and interesting reading for you. More importantly, I hope you picked up at least one tip or technique that will make you more successful. If you have gotten just one idea from this book that will help you become more productive, then I have accomplished what I set out to do, and you have invested your time wisely. If you like the book and you think the tips and ideas were beneficial, **tell your friends to go and buy a copy**. If you don't like the book and you think it is detrimental to your success, **tell your competitors to go buy a copy**.

Either way, I win. That's what selling is all about: bringing an opportunity to a close where everyone feels like he wins. If you aren't already, you can be a part of this proud, challenging and rewarding profession.

GOOD LUCK
and
GOOD SELLING!

APPENDIX A

ATTENTION-GETTERS

- I am _____ from _____. I work as a consultant to the _____ industry. I'm here today to see if there is a way for _____ and your company to increase your competitive posture, your efficiency and your profits.

- If I could show you how having _____ as a business partner can save you time and money, would you spend some time discussing your business with me?

- How would you like to have an all-expense-paid trip for two to Hawaii? In the next 20 minutes, I will show you how you can have it.

- I would like to offer you a dream vacation for the price of taking a family of four to a baseball game.

- I've been working with _____ for two years now. Aren't they a competitor of yours? The product they bought from me has helped them to reduce their inventory by 25 percent and increase sales by 7 percent through better customer information. I know I can do the same for you. May I have a few minutes of your time to discuss the opportunity for your business?

- I do not want to talk to you today about (your product). I want to talk to you about solutions to business problems that can save or make you money.

- I would like to introduce you to a new drug that will cure _____ without leaving side effects.

- Hello Mr. ___. My name is __ from _____. I want to thank you for taking time to see me today. I understand that you are willing to talk to anyone that can help you increase revenue within your business. I would like to tell you about my new product that can do just that.

- I have an idea that will revolutionize the _____ industry.

- I am an insurance consultant. My specialty has been finding executives just like you who desire to increase revenues. Can I please gather some facts in the next few minutes that would help me determine if I can help you?

- The fuel consumption on this automobile is 35 percent less than its closest competition.

- I recently installed a new automated pumping system nearby. The president of that organization challenged me to help him increase his bottom line. Through a few short meetings, we found the right solution to his needs. Do you have a few minutes to see if I can do the same for you?

- I'm here to show you how my product can be a cost-effective and profitable investment for your company.

- If I could show you a way you could increase your company's profits by 15 percent, would you spend the afternoon discussing my ideas on the golf course?

- Mr. ___, I'm a _____ specialist. I have been very successful over the past years ____ working with companies like yours, making them more competitive within the industry. Are you interested in becoming more competitive?

- I would like to show you a new product that can produce the same amount of work as four people at half the cost.

- If my program could help your medical practice become more efficient, increase your cash flow and generate more new patients for less than minimum wage, would you be interested in discussing it?

- I would like to discuss how my company has helped companies similar to yours increase productivity and sales while reducing labor costs. Are you interested?

- Hello, my name is ___. I am a salesman for ____ and I am here to help you make money.

- Hello, my name is _____. I am a specialist in the ____ industry. I'm here to discuss ways to help you better manage your company.

- With this policy, should you ever become disabled, you will never have to worry about being able to maintain your current standard of living.

- Did you spend more time last night than you wanted worrying about your business?

- I have been working with the Smith Company. Joe Smith suggested I stop in and spend a few minutes with you.

- I would like to take a few minutes to discuss with you some of the cost-effective new technologies we offer – technologies that can help your company become more competitive and profitable.

- I would like to take five minutes to determine if a relationship between your company and mine could be profitable.

- I would like to have 10 minutes of your time. It is important to both of us.

- Does making more profit next year get your attention?

- Is your business running to suit you?

- Mr. Jones, why did you agree to see me today?

- I would like to show you how to increase your market share with little impact on your expenses.

- How would you like to have a three-day weekend for the rest of your working career?

- I would like to take a few minutes to discuss the critical vulnerability your company is facing in today's marketplace and how we can help you take measures to reduce your exposure.

- According to a national association of _____, your competitors will spend 3 to 5 percent of their gross income to try to take your customers away from you. Do you have a few minutes to discuss how we can create barriers for your competition if they move on your customers?

- Sam suggested that competition was making inroads into your customer base. I would like to talk to you about ways to prevent that.

- Do you have the level of customer satisfaction that you would like to have?

- If I can show you how to make more money, will you see me for five minutes?

- My name is _____. I have two jobs, to represent my company to you and to represent you to my company. May I have five minutes of your time?

- If I could put money in your pocket, would you give me a few minutes of your time to show you how?

- I am new in the area, and I wanted to see what makes you so successful. (You are really looking for a weakness.)

- I am _____ with ____. We have had the opportunity to help some of your fellow owners solve their labor relations problems. Is this something you would be interested in discussing?

- My name is ___ with ____ Company. You may have heard that our company installed the cooling system for the _____ Company.

- I'm _____ from ___. We specialize in the insurance industry. I'm here to show you a way to help you keep up with all the changes in the industry.

- I am __ with the ___ Corporation, and I am here to discuss with you ways to generate additional revenue for your company through the use of _____.

- Would you like to increase your profits by 25 percent in the next 12 months?

- We've helped companies like yours right here in the _____ area improve their profits.

- I am going to save you money while keeping you ahead of your competition.

- Hello. I'm ____. I am from ___. I'd like to talk to you today about improving customer satisfaction.

- Hello, I'm _____ and I'm here today representing ____ in the hospitality industry. I'd like to talk to you about increasing occupancy rates.

- I would like to show you a way to reduce your workmen's compensation expense by closely tracking work categories.

- This fabric will change the way people think about wearing winter coats.

- Good morning, my name is _____ with ____ . I would like to introduce you to _____ products that can help increase profits and cut costs.

- I would like to show you a product that can help your business increase profitability.

- My name is _____, your ____ marketing representative. I'm here today to show you how ____ can help you make money.

- My name is ___ with _____. I'm here to discuss ways in which our company may assist you in generating more revenue and controlling costs.

- My name is _____, with ____, and I am here today to save you at least $15,000 a year.

- My name is _____. I am here to help you get an edge on the competition.

- I would like to talk to you about controlling costs and increasing profitability through the use of computers.

- I would like to talk to you about ways to grow your business. I would like to talk to you about how top performers in your industry are using our technology.

- I would like to talk to you about your expectations of our company.

- I would like to talk to you about how our products are helping companies in your industry.

- I am here to talk to you about ways that you can become more competitive.

- I would like to talk to you about trends and directions of the _____ industry and how our company is playing an active role in that process.

- I would like to talk to you about new uses for _____ in your industry.

- I am here to help you address your top priorities, exceed your goals and make your financial measurements.

- My name is _____, with _____. I have a financing plan that will allow you to acquire basically anything you would like.

- I am a marketing consultant from _____. I work with small and intermediate businesses to help them find ways to improve cash flow, reduce operating expenses and improve profitability.

- I would like to give you some ideas how companies in your industry are leveraging technology to improve the operations of their businesses.

- I would like to talk to you about new business opportunities for your company.

- Did you worry as much about your business last night as I did?

- I would like to talk to you about the expenditure of your _____ budget.

- I am about to introduce you to an automobile that will set the standards for _____.

- I would like to talk to you about ways to increase student test scores.

- I would like to spend 15 minutes with you exploring ways we can help you save money.

- I would like to talk to you about an investment that has increased many of our customers' competitive edge.

- I would like to talk to you about information systems and how they can save make money.

- I would like to talk to you about ways to increase the productivity of your people.

- If I could reduce your inventory cost by 30 percent, would you be willing to sit down for a few minutes and talk with me?

- I would like to talk to you about how I can assist you in meeting your business goals.

- I would like to help you make money.

- Is your business making as much money as it could for you today?

- I would like to talk to you about increasing the quality of your product.

- I would like to present to you the most effective business solution for your company.

- My purpose in being here is to help you make more money. If you are not interested, let me know now. If you are interested, let me take 30 minutes.

- My manager told me that I should meet you ... I want to find out why.

- I'm an industry specialist managing a team of industry experts. I would like to show you how my team can make your company more competitive in today's challenging market.

- I am here to show you how I have been able to help your competitors increase revenue and improve customer service.

- I would like 10 minutes to share some new ideas with you and to determine your interest in my service.

- For a limited time only, I can save you _____ percent on the price of our product.

- I have a once-in-a-lifetime opportunity for you.

- I am here to talk about _____.

- I am calling to make you aware of _____.

- I am here to talk about how we can make money.

- I know how valuable your time is, so I will get right to the point.

- I would like to know if you would have any interest in discussing some ideas that have proven to be successful for other companies like yours.

- I am with _____. We have been working with a consultant who has identified your company as one who has a great need for _____ in the near future. Would you give me a few minutes to understand your requirements and to determine if I can be of help to both you and your company?

- I was reading about your company's goals in the newspaper. Would like to discuss some ways that I might help you achieve those goals more quickly. Do you have a few minutes?

- Let's try that again. Hi, I am _____ from _____. (You can use this if someone cuts you off right up front or throws you out.)

- You don't know me, and I don't know you. However, if things go well during the next few minutes, you are going to be one of my favorite people.

APPENDIX B

TIPS FOR SUCCESS

1. Call On The **PRESIDENT** First!

2. Call On The **TOP DECISION MAKER**!

3. Observe The Guest Sign-In Register To Check For Mutual Friends In Common, Competitors, Etc.

4. Understand That The Prospect **Must Buy You** Before Buying Your Product

5. Sell Yourself

6. Develop A Positive Relationship With The Prospect Or Customer

7. Be Punctual

8. Be Prepared

9. Look Successful

10. Be In Command

11. Show Enthusiasm About Your Product, Service And Company

12. Be Confident

13. Be Optimistic

14. Be A Good Listener

15. Show Sincere Concern

16. Be Attentive

17. Be Poised

18. Be Patient

19. Be Positive

20. Be Articulate

21. Be Knowledgeable

22. Ensure That Your Customers Or Prospects **DO NOT** Know More About Your Company Than You Do

23. Ensure That Your Customers Or Prospects **DO NOT** Know More About Your Product Than You Do

24. Ensure That Your Customers Or Prospects **DO NOT** Know More About Your Business Than You Do

25. Get In Tune With Your Prospect's Needs, Wants And Desires

26. Believe You Are Needed

27. Believe You Offer Opportunity

28. Be Viewed As A Consultant

29. Be A Solution Provider

30. Be A Problem Solver

31. Sell To The Level Of The Buyer

32. Paint A Picture, Keep It Simple

33. Be Empathetic!!!

34. Stick To The Issue At Hand

35. Don't Ramble – Net It Out

36. Never Assume You Will Or Will Not Get The Sale

37. Never Assume People Are Competent

38. Ask The Tough Questions Up Front

39. Sell The **Benefits**

40. Focus On **Investing** In Your Product And Not Just Buying

41. Focus On Cost Versus Price

42 Be Thick-Skinned And Tenacious

43. Watch For Buying Signals

44. Understand The Politics Behind The Buying Decision

45. Never Accept "We Are Happy With The Way Things Are"

46. Never Accept "We Have No Problems"

47. Never Accept A Bad Economy As A Reason Not To Buy

48. Never Talk Up Or Down To People

49. Don't Treat Prospects Or Customers Like Children

50. Don't Manipulate Your Prospect

51. Realize That How You Say It Is As Important As What You Say

52. If You Don't Know the Answer, Say You Don't Know But You Will Find Out

53. Respond Quickly To Any Request

54. Do What You Say You Are Going To Do And **More**

55. Network

56. Eat Lunch With Prospects And Customers

57. Make Certain As Many People As Possible In The Account Know You

58. Be Courteous

59. Remember, You Are An Outsider When You Are On the Prospect's Turf – Respect His Way Of Doing Things

60. Treat Everyone In The Organization With Respect

61. Have Integrity

62. Finish Your To-Do's Ahead Of Time

63. Have Other People **Wanting** To Work With You

64. Work Smart, Not Hard

65. Expect The Unexpected

66. Be A Team Player

67. Always Be Alert To Opportunity

68. Don't Park In The Prospect's Reserved Parking Spaces

69. Don't Burn Bridges